Hearing *a* Voice
and
the Voice

Andrew C. Phiri

miTe
Publishing

PO Box 37919 • Lusaka - Zambia

Hearing *a* Voice and *the* Voice
A compilation of sermons

Copyright © 2018 Andrew C. Phiri
www.andrewcphiri.com | voiceoftheword@live.com

Printed in USA
Published by MiTe Publishing Ltd

ISBN-13: 978-9982-9986-4-2
ISBN-10: 9982-9986-4-1

Unless otherwise indicated all scripture quotations were taken from the Holy Bible - King James Version © Cambridge University Press.

FREE COPIES OF THIS BOOK ARE AVAILABLE

If you can't afford buying this book send a request for a free copy to voiceoftheword@live.com. However, please note that free copies can only be sent when resources are available. The list of requests for free books is often long, making it difficult to send books as soon as you may desire them.

To
the elect lady and her children, whom I
love in the truth, and not I only, but also
all they that have known the truth
(2 Joh.1:1).

Contents

1.	Vanity	5
2.	And the books were opened	13
3.	Proud but knowing nothing	19
4.	Adding to the Word	30
5.	Looking but not Seeing	41
6.	In the Name of Jesus	61
7.	Finding fault	82
8.	Hearing the voice of God	109
9.	That every mouth be stopped	116
10.	Shadows	123
11.	Overcoming by Grace	129
12.	Throw away the sticks	139
13.	How camest thou in?	146

1.

Vanity

"For the word of God is quick, and powerful, and sharper than any two-edged sword, piercing even to the dividing asunder of soul and spirit, and of the joints and marrow, and is a discerner of the thoughts and intents of the heart"

Heb.4:12

I thought I had arrived at a clinic or a hospital of some sort when I saw the immense structure of the estate. We had been picked from home to pray for a patient. I didn't know the people but they somewhat heard about our ministry.

Passing through the living room its opulence was quite an attraction. There was a fountain of water in the centre of the room. In the beautiful sofas around the walls were several relatives; the elderly and young, all in a sombre mood. We proceeded to the bedroom.

We stood a few centimetres from the bed as we waited for the patient to be brought in. We were surprised when an elderly woman, mother to the patient, went close to the bed and rolled-off the thick blanket. There the rich man lay! Thin and without strength, he spoke in desperation: "Pastor, please pray for me, I don't want to die!"

The desperation I saw in his eyes have forever remained in my memory.

The patient had clearly been a man

of status but in that moment the pending loss of all his labours stared in his face. However, an imminent greater loss should have been his fear.

Loss of the Soul

A crack in the wall is mended by cement, a substance from which it was made. Generally speaking a thing is sustained by the substance from which it was made.

In the beginning God commanded the earth to bring forth plants and it was so. A tree grew and hence lived from the soil it came from. Uproot a tree from the soil and it will soon wither and perish!

God spoke to the waters to bring forth fish and it was so. Take a fish out of water and it will die!

When it was time to make man, God, that Almighty Spirit, looked into Himself and brought forth man, created in His *image* and *enclosed* in a body of clay. Thus, man was a soul endowed with the spirit of life – a *"living **soul**"* (Gen.2:7).

The soul is what a person is – his thoughts, imaginations, and consciousness. You are aware that you exist because you are a soul. That awareness is possible because of the spirit of life. Thus, without the spirit of life, a person's consciousness of being in existence would simply vanish! Right now you are able to think and reason, and are aware that you are alive because your soul has the spirit of life.

Now, the soul (with the spirit of life in it) dwells in the body of flesh. Through the body we interact with the physical world. However, the body is only a house in which the real you (the soul) dwells. That house can easily be disengaged from the soul (cf. 2 Cor.5:1-2). A sword – knife, gun, poison, or whatever dangerous object or situation - can easily cause the separation of the soul from the body. When that happens we say a person has died. The owner of the body suffers loss of whatever wealth he or she may have accrued in this world. In that moment all carnal things become unprofitable to the soul! That is a loss but not so great a loss as one that involves losing one self's consciousness, i.e. losing the soul! In Mark 8:36 The Lord Jesus admonished, *"For what shall it profit a man, if he shall gain the whole world, and **lose his own soul?"***

First and Second Death

From the death of the first man on this earth (Abel) to this day, all who have died have only experienced what we identify as the **First Death** in Scriptures.

As was earlier indicated, during the First Death the human soul loses its 'clothing' of the body. The soul becomes naked, so to speak. This occurs when the soul, together with the intrinsic spirit of life in it, departs from the body. Like we read concerning Rachel, *"it came to pass, as her soul was in departing (for she died)"* (Gen.35:18).

It is the earnest hope of a true believer that one day when his body (called *"earthly house"* or *"tabernacle"* in 2 Cor.5:1) dies, at the day of the resurrection he shall be clothed again when he rises with a glorified body (2 Cor.5:3-4).

As earlier stated above, the death of the body can be caused by man's 'sword'. That is a terrible thing to happen and we all try to escape from being killed. That is why there are policemen and hospitals in every country. They are there to guard against the death of the flesh. However, people should be more afraid of the greater and more fearsome loss, the loss of the soul! This loss can never be caused by man's sword. Not even Satan can cause it!

The loss of the soul is called the death of the soul. In the book of Revelation it is referred to as the **Second Death**. It involves the separation of the spirit of life from a person's soul. When that happens, a person would literally vanish, i.e. go out of existence, leaving behind *"neither root nor branch"* (Mal.4:1). Like the Lord Jesus taught, only God can cause the death of the soul – *"fear not them which* **kill the body**, *but are not able to* **kill the soul**: *but rather fear* *him which is able to destroy **both soul** and **body** in hell"* (Mat.10:28).

So, there is the destruction of the body (when the soul and its spirit of life leaves the body) and also the destruction of the soul (when the spirit of life departs from the soul). The latter can only be caused by the Sword of God, *"For the word of God is quick, and powerful, and **sharper than any two-edged sword**, piercing even to the **dividing asunder of soul and spirit**"* (Heb.4:12).

When Paul in Hebrews 4:12 says *"sharper than any two-edged sword"*, it is another way of saying, "no weapon of man can cause the death of the soul; only God's Sword can separate the spirit of life from the soul." God's Sword is His Word. It is the power of this Word which will one day destroy all forces of Darkness - *"And the beast was taken, and with him the false prophet that wrought miracles before him, with which he deceived them that had received the mark of the beast, and them that worshipped his image. These both were cast alive into a lake of fire burning with brimstone. And the remnant* *were slain with the sword of him that sat upon the horse, **which sword proceeded out of his mouth**: and all the fowls were filled with their flesh"* (Rev.19:20-21).

Notice that just like the Lord Jesus had indicated in Matthew 10:28, apostle John saw a vision which indicated that the Second Death will occur in Hell after judgement: *"And the sea gave up the dead which were in it; and death and hell delivered up the dead which were in them: and they were judged every man according to their works. And death and hell were cast into the lake of fire. This is **the second death**"* (Rev.20:13-14).

Surely to live through a bountiful life but which finally ends up in not only losing your earthly posessions but your very own existence would be a huge loss! That would ultimately reduce all that you pursued in life to vanity!

2.

And the books were opened...

"And I saw the dead, small and great, stand before God; and the books were opened, and another book was opened, which is the book of life, and the dead were judged out of those things which were written in the books, according to their works"

Rev.20:12

When I was a little boy I used to think that there was a big book in heaven called the *Book of Life* where names of good people were recorded. And when I read Revelation 3:5 I believed that when a person did something bad his or her name would be rubbed from the book.

It is important to know that the book of Revelation was written in symbols. In one place we read about a lamb having *"seven horns and seven eyes"* sitting on a throne. There is surely no such animal in heaven. Neither is there a wild animal called *"lion from the tribe of Judah"*. It goes without saying that there is also no clerical department where records of sinners and saints get regularly updated!

As human beings we write to keep a record of something so that we don't forget it. This enables us to preserve information for reference purposes. Because of this the invention of ink and paper have been very useful. Now, God is not man that He should forget and be reminded by a written record. Neither is heaven a natural place that it should be stocked with paper files. So then, what are the *"books"* and the *"book of life"* in Revelation 20:12?

Living epistles

A true believer has God's Word abiding in his or her heart. The life of that Word manifests in them. *"Ye are our epistle written in our hearts, known and read of all men"* Paul wrote to the Ephesian believers (2 Cor.3:2). An unbeliever is also a 'book'.

See, we are on a journey through time. In this journey we have found ourselves equipped with the *ink* of blood and the *pen* of life and are to write a story on the *pages* of time.

Think about how far you have come in life. How old are you? What story have you been writing this far? What's been the theme of your story? How many *pages* do you think are remaining before your covers close? If today your covers close, what will the owner of the ink and pages say about your story – "a waste", "meaningless", or "well done, my good and faithful servant"?

One can either write a story of his own "works" – his achievements and successes – or of the will of the owner of the ink and paper. It is important to know that the ink of blood and pages of time are not our resources and it isn't just a wise thing to get started with a life story for which we don't know the purpose or destination. Apostle Paul was wise. He died to himself and chose to let Christ live through him. "*For to me to live is Christ*" (Phi.1:21). So, Paul wasn't writing his own story. He was dead to himself and chose to live and manifest the Life of the Word. Like Paul, all true believers' lives are dead to themselves and their life is hid with Christ in God – "*For ye are dead, and your life is hid with Christ in God*" (Col.3:3). Their names are in the Book of Life, which is the Word of God! Because of this, they shall never be judged during the White Throne Judgment.

In Revelation 20:12, the "*books*" shall be judged by "*the Book of Life*". So, if one doesn't have a book (life) of his own, but his *name* (life) is in the Book of Life, he will be the one to judge the world. "*Do ye not know that the saints shall judge the world?*" (1 Cor.6:3). To this agrees the words of the Lord Jesus when He said, "*Verily, verily, I say unto you, He that heareth my word, and believeth on him that sent me, hath everlasting life, and shall not come into condemnation; but is passed from death unto life*" (Joh.5:24).

One day your book will close!

One thing is certain, one day you will put a final stroke on your last page, the covers will close, and you will be shelved away from the land of the living. But…"*the books were opened*"… the eyes of Saint John saw the vision; "*and another book was opened, which is the book of life: and the dead were judged out of those things which were written in the books, according to their works. And the sea gave up the dead which were in it; and death and hell delivered up the dead which were in them: and they were judged every man according to their works"* (Rev.20:12-13).

Surely a day of reckoning is coming when you will have to account for how you used the 'ink' of life and 'pages' of your earthly days. *"So teach us to number our days, that we may apply our hearts unto wisdom"* prayed the psalmist. (Psa.90:12).

3.

Proud but knowing nothing

"He is proud, knowing nothing, but doting about questions and strifes of words, whereof cometh envy, strife, railings, evil surmisings, perverse disputings of men of corrupt minds, and destitute of the truth, supposing that gain is godliness, from such withdraw thyself"

1 Tim.6:4

Blessed is he that receives spiritual knowledge. We say "receives" because this knowledge can only be given by God. And the knowledge that God gives is not for merely fulfilling an intellectual curiosity. The knowledge God gives is not for one person to feel smarter than another person. It is not a theoretical concept but a transforming power – "*In the beginning was the Word…In Him was life…as many as received Him, to them gave He **power to become the sons of God**"* (Joh.1:1,4,12).

Natural Knowledge

Natural knowledge can inform a person how to properly construct sentences in English. He or she will learn about vowels, plurals, verbs, and adjectives. Natural knowledge will teach you how to indicate in a certain portion of writing that certain words you used were quoted from a certain source. It will teach you how to appropriately quote and cite words 'according to the *Harvard referencing style*'.

Natural knowledge will inform you

that the word "***this***" is a *pronoun* and, as explained by the Cambridge Advanced Learners Dictionary is "*used for a person, object, idea, etc. to show **which one is referred to**"*.

That day when Jesus was at the temple and said "*Destroy **this** temple, and in three days I will raise it up*" (Joh.2:19), the 'knowledgeable' men had every reason to raise what seemed a sound argument against him – "*Forty and six years was **this** temple in building, and wilt thou rear it up in three days?*" (Joh.2:20). Yes, Jesus was at the temple that day and his "this", grammatically speaking, could only refer to the physical structure of the building. That's the only temple the people with him could see! The people took the issue seriously. To them Jesus had ridiculed or insulted the one holy place which was central to Judaism.

Jesus was brought before the council of chief priests and elders (These are what you may call bishops and reverends in Christian religious establishments). Then some witnesses came forth to testify of what they heard Jesus speak about the temple. They spoke, *"This fellow said, I am able to destroy the temple of God, and to build it in three days"* (Mat.26:61).

Was their testimony true? Yes, according to what their natural ears heard and what the pronouns, nouns and verbs meant in the words of Jesus. If tape-recorders were available to supplement the evidence, the accusers would have happily indicted Him with 'saying what the *tape* says'!

However, *saying what the tape says* does not always amount to speaking what it meant! It is little wonder that Matthew called those accusers of Jesus *"false witnesses"*! They could speak the words of Jesus but their understanding of what He meant was as far as the East is from West.

Jesus was talking about the temple of his body, how he would die and on the third rise to life. His accusers were thinking about the physical temple. I have to say, even myself, despite all the love I have for Jesus, I would have never grasped what the Lord meant had God not opened my understanding!

Now think of it, just how many "false witnesses" do we have on pulpits today; witnesses who try to quote Scripture word-for-word but yet never grasping the mind of God behind the written Words? Just how many false witnesses do we have telling the story that Adam and Eve ate some food they were not supposed to and hence the problems of sickness, war, and all the turmoil of the world?

If death merely came by eating a literal fruit wouldn't redemption come by eating from a literal *Tree of Life*! Why should it come by a man being born without sex, and through that having clean blood which should cleanse us from our contaminated one (Psa.51:5)? And is it not because of the contaminated state of our blood that we should be "born again"(Joh. 3:3)?

The Bible's story of redemption,

which revolves around the Blood of Jesus, can never be truly grasped without an understanding of what sin happened in Eden, a sin that made God curse the sexual organ of a woman to experience pain when giving birth. One needs eyes to see the life 'behind' the letters of Scripture! When one beholds the *life*, he or she will see the coherent story of redemption that unfolds from Genesis through Revelation.

The wise and the foolish

*"The tongue of the wise **utters knowledge rightly**"* said King Solomon, *"but the mouth of **self-confident fools** pours out folly"* (Pro.15:2, Amplified Bible).

Notice what makes some people wise – they know how to use or apply knowledge. So, merely having knowledge of something doesn't make you wise; you have to know it "rightly" by knowing what *this* means and where *that* applies. It is for this same reason that apostle Paul admonished Timothy telling him to *"study to show thyself approved unto God, a workman that needeth* *not to be ashamed, **rightly dividing the word of truth**. But shun **profane and vain babblings**: for they will increase unto more ungodliness"* (2 Tim.2:15).

Watch the last words of the above verse – *"profane and vain babblings"*! Someone may gather a little information from some book and, without giving careful thought to the depth of facts, he may begin to think of himself as a master of a subject. He then begins to attack those people he feels are ignorant about what he knows. When he speaks to undiscerning minds, his words may sound interesting, but when trained eyes and ears observe, what they behold is a soul gone into *"vain jangling"* (1 Tim.1:6), speaking *"evil of those things which they know not, but what they know naturally, as brute beasts, in those things they corrupt themselves"* (Jud.10).

Talk of brute beasts, there are men who are as bold as lions in fighting what they think is error. Paul was once such a man, persecuting what he believed was a cult misleading people from the true faith of Judaism. But one day that light struck him and when he was prayed for scales came off his eyes. Only then did he see the truth of the Word he had been fighting.

Condemning Branham and Moses

In the year 2016, whilst in India, I saw a man *"jangling"* over some words. He was talking about William Branham and Moses.

He condemned Branham to have added words to the Scripture and warned the audience of how anyone who does that would be condemned to God's plagues and judgements. With boldness and emotion the man read a verse from the book of Revelation 10:7 which says, *"But in the days of the voice of the seventh angel, when he shall begin to sound, the mystery of God should be finished, as he hath declared to his servants the prophets."* He denounced what William Branham often said about this verse, that the angel in the verse would reveal "all mysteries".

In an emotional tone the man

warned: "What does the Bible say in the last chapter of Revelation…if you take one word out of prophecy…your name shall be taken from the Book of Life!" He was referring to Revelation 22:19 to emphasise that instead of quoting the word *"finished"* Branham introduced "revealed."

The anti-Branham preacher next cited Moses of the Bible to have also erred by changing the Word of God. He explained that because of the offense, God forbade the Hebrew prophet from entering the promised land! According to him when Moses smote the rock, instead of speaking to it, he changed the Word from *"speak"* to *"smite"*.

Next he was out to show that what Branham preached as the revelation of Seven Seals was not God-given as per his testimony but a message copied from Dr Clarence Larkin's book. Larkin's work is titled the *Book of Revelation* and was written some 40 years earlier before William Branham's preaching on the subject. The anti-

Branham preacher spoke these words:

> **Everything** that's been written by Clarence Larkin **in this book** [*pointing to Larkin's book*] **is in the Seven Seals book** [*of William Branham*]. Check it! What is this? **Is that revelation from the seven angels?**[1]

This accusation of plagiarism should be of profound concern to all those, like me, who believe in the ministry and teachings of William Branham. If the allegation is true then we are of all Christians the most duped and deceived! However, if objective and irrefutable evidence shall be given in this message, that the critic's assertions are not only uninformed but a twist of facts with intent to deceive, then a fool is walking with hobnailed shoes on grounds where angels would fear to tread!

Sitting in the audience and looking at the man's emotional speaking everyone should have seen that the man seemed sincere in his zeal. However, as

---

[1] Transcribed from audio recording.

we will shortly see, sincerity does not define truth.

4.

Adding to the Word?

"In the beginning was the Word, and the Word was with God, and the Word was God…In him was life; and the life was the light of men"

Joh. 1:1,4

They were three. Humble-looking elderly men, so fluent in quoting Bible verses. Jehovah's Witnesses. In the course of our discussion I asked them:

"Tell me, if Adam and Eve merely ate a literal fruit, why did God curse the woman's sexual organ in Genesis 3:16 so that she should experience pain when giving birth? With God, it's *"an eye for an eye"* and *"tooth for a tooth"*[2], and so, why didn't He instead curse Eve's mouth or intestines with some sort of ulcers?"

"Tell me, what would you suspect in a court room where three accused persons with downcast faces - *Mr A, Mrs A* and *Mr B* – are standing before a judge and you hear him sternly cautioning *Mrs A* to subject her desire (passion, longing) to her husband? What has 'desire to your husband' got to do with eating an *apple*?"

"Tell me why Paul in 2 Corinthians 11:1-3 would be talking about a

---

[2] Exodus 21:23-25.

marriage issue between Christ and His espoused wife and then admonishes the wife to be faithful to her husband not as Eve who was beguiled by the serpent? How inappropriate would such a comparison be?"

"Why was the redemption of the human race to come through a person not born through sex? Why was He to have pure blood? Does this not mean the Original Sin involved an act which polluted human blood, causing a disturbance in the genes of humanity? Isn't that the reason for the need to be *born again*?"

I told the three gentlemen in plain words:

"Can't you see that the Original Sin committed in Eden involved an act of adultery between the woman and Mr Serpent?"

They had never heard the doctrine before. It was too incongruent with their doctrines. One of them responded:

"No, that can't be! To say the Original Sin was adultery would be adding to the Scripture! If it were so, the word adultery would have been stated in Genesis chapter 3. If it was adultery the Bible would have stated it plainly."

I could not help but intrude into their territory of cherished but most misleading teachings; I answered:

"Well then, in your book *Pay Attention to Daniel's Prophecy*, pages 94 and 95, you explain something interesting about the immense tree in the dream of Nebuchadnezzar. Although Daniel clearly interpreted the tree to refer to Nebuchadnezzar as the mighty king of Babylon, in your book you went further to explain that 'the tree stands for rulership and sovereignty far grander than that of Babylon's king. It symbolizes the universal sovereignty of Jehovah, *the King of the heavens*, especially with respect to the earth.' You then stated that the 'kingdom' was centred in Jerusalem, 'with David and his heirs sitting on *Jehovah's throne*'. Thus, in your interpretation the cutting down of the tree occurred when Jerusalem was destroyed by the Babylonians. So, tell me, Did you add to the words of Daniel by introducing an interpretation which is completely absent in his explanation of the dream?"

There was a long pause. The three men looked at each trying to decide who would respond to my question. One of them finally slowly answered:

"Well, God progressively reveals His Word!"

"Right", I agreed; "and I am here to tell you that the progressive revelation about the Eden story is that adultery was involved in the Original Sin!" [3]

One elder looked at the wall clock in the house, as another checked his wrist watch:

"Oh, it's already lunch time! I think we can continue this discussion next time."

It's been 17 years ago and I am still

---

[3] My agreement was to the statement on 'progressive revelation', not their misinterpretation of Nebuchadnezzar's dream of the immense tree.

waiting for the three men.

If the meaning of "adding to Scripture" is as has been given by anti-Branham preachers, or the Jehovah Witness elders I conversed with, we will find ourselves not only throwing away what Branham taught, but the New Testament Bible altogether! Indeed, on account of the supposed discrepancies, there are many people today who have refused to regard the New Testament as inspired Scripture.

The faulty definition of 'adding to Scripture' has led many Jewish rabbis and Muslim scholars to denounce New Testament scriptures as being uninspired. According to them, New Testament authors quoted many Old Testament scriptures out of context and in doing that they also introduced words not found in the supposed referenced verses.

Matthew quoting Scripture out of context?

The Gospel of Matthew tells us that when Joseph fled to Egypt with Jesus, running away from Herod, that was a fulfilment of Hosea 11:1 – *"he took the young child and his mother by night, and departed into Egypt: and he was there until the death of Herod that it might be fulfilled which was spoken of the Lord by the prophet, saying, Out of Egypt have I called my son"*(Mat.2:14). However, when we turn to the book of Hosea itself, we find a story that was clearing talking about the exodus of Jews from Egypt. In stating this historical event Hosea's prophecy refers to Israel as God's son. Here are the words: *"When Israel was a child, then I loved him, and called my son out of Egypt."* So Matthew has been accused to be guilty of quoting and misapplying Scripture. Let's go to Luke.

Luke *"adding"* to the Scripture?

The Gospel of Luke in one place is supposed to have quoted word-for-word a passage from Isaiah 61:1-2 which says: *"The spirit of the Lord GOD is upon me; because the LORD hath anointed me to preach good tidings unto the meek; he hath sent me to bind up the broken-hearted, to proclaim liberty to the captives, and the opening of the prison to them that are bound*". But in the Gospel according to Luke, Jesus read the same words of Isaiah 61:1-2 as follows: "*The Spirit of the Lord is upon me, because he hath anointed me to preach the gospel to the poor; he hath sent me to heal the broken-hearted, to preach deliverance to the captives, **and recovering of sight to the blind**, to set at liberty them that are bruised, To preach the acceptable year of the Lord.*"

The words "*recovering of sight to the blind*" are clearly not found in Isaiah. So, did Jesus or Luke add to the Scripture?

Paul is the one author heavily criticized for changing, altering and misquoting Old Testament scriptures. In Ephesians 4:11 he supposedly quoted Psalm 68:18 when he wrote, "*Wherefore he saith, When he ascended up on high, he led captivity captive, and **gave gifts unto men**.*" However, it turns out that the actual words in Psalm 68:18 read: "*Thou hast ascended on high, thou hast led captivity captive: **thou hast received gifts for men***; *yea, for the rebellious also, that the*

LORD God might dwell among them."

The sentences *"gave gifts unto men"* and *"received gifts for men"* are quite very opposite in meaning, scholars have said.

The Lord Jesus not spared by the critics

The Lord Jesus is not spared from the criticism. He once said that the Jewish people of the Exodus did not eat of the true bread of heaven and hence they died. He then presented Himself as the bread that came from heaven – *"I am that bread of life. Your fathers did eat manna in the wilderness, and are dead.* **This is the bread which cometh down from heaven,** *that a man may eat thereof, and not die"* (Joh.6:48-49). Jesus seems to have directly contradicted Psalm 78:23-25, *"He had commanded the clouds from above, and opened the doors of heaven, And had rained down manna upon them to eat, and had given them of the corn of heaven. Man did eat angels' food: he sent them meat to the full."*

Jesus is further accused by rabbis to have encouraged people to break the law. To-date they believe that he was a false Messiah. Rabbi Shraga Simmons notes:

> The Messiah will lead the Jewish people to full Torah observance…Throughout the Christian "New Testament", Jesus contradicts the Torah and states that its commandments are no longer applicable. For example, John 9:14 records that Jesus made a paste in violation of Shabbat, which caused the Pharisees to say (verse 16), *"He does not observe Shabbat!"*[4]

These are the same accusations that led to Christ being crucified.

Adding to the Torah?

In Deuteronomy chapters 4 and 12 God warned the Israelites not to add to the law he had given them. He told them, *"Ye shall not add unto the word which I command you, neither shall ye diminish ought from it, that ye may keep the commandments of the LORD your God which I command you"* (Deu.4:2). Does

---

[4] Simmons, S. (2004). *Why Jews don't Believe in Jesus.* [Online] available from: http://www.aish.com/jw/s/48892792.html [Accessed: 3 February 2018].

this mean that all other writings that came after the first five books of Moses were an addition to Scripture and should never be regarded to be inspired? What exactly does it to mean to add or to subtract from the Scripture?

5.
Looking but not Seeing

" And he looked up, and said, I see men as trees, walking. After that he put his hands again upon his eyes, and made him look up: and he was restored, and saw every man clearly"

Mar. 8:24-25

I am not a grandpa but I do love to tell some bed-time tales to my children. Here is one.

The farmer and the Stranger

Once upon a time there was a farmer who was visited by a stranger from another planet. The stranger was bewildered at the sight of beautiful mango trees.

"Back home we don't have such tall structures with those green platters (he meant *leaves!*) and round balls (he meant *mangoes!*) which taste so sweet in the mouth!" the stranger exclaimed.

"Well", the farmer began to explain as he stooped down to pick a dry mango seed: "You can take this to your planet. Plant it in the soil and you will also have the nice sight of trees with their beautiful leaves and mango fruits!"

Baffled, the stranger asked: "What is that supposed to mean?"

"Well, what you are looking at in my hands is called a seed. It has a trunk inside! It has the beautiful green leaves inside! It has the sweet mangoes in it! Inside this one seed there is a big forest of trees!"

"Am confused at what you are saying!" the stranger marveled. "I can only see a small round dry object in your hands!"

"Well, for you to see what I am talking about you have to put this seed in the ground, water it, and let the sun shine upon it" the farmer tried to explain.

"Is that supposed to be a joke? I am a big person and you are here telling me tales?" the stranger angrily dismissed the farmer's explanation.

"Well, we can only settle the argument if you try out what I am telling you."

It was evening and the two bid each other farewell. The stranger went with the mango seed to go and examine it under a microscope, peradventure there was some truth to the odd explanation.

Sitting alone he probed further. He sliced the seed and put it under a microscope. He hoped to see tiny images of trees under the lens. "I am too old to be fooled!" he grumbled as he threw away the seed and forgave himself for having been silly to act on what was supposed to be a stupid joke.

Looking

The stranger failed to see the leaves because he was looking at the *form* of the seed and how its shape and appearance was so different from the beautiful mango trees.

Shape of a mango seed

He could not see any similarity between a dry ovoid seed and the elongated structure of a trunk with its clusters of beautiful fresh leaves!

Sight showed him that the objects were unrelated. If the stranger would have gone further to examine the difference between the tastes of a mango seed, fruit, and leaves, he would have found them to be completely unrelated. Thus, reliance on his five senses would be so deceptive.

Shape of a tree

The stranger had tried to investigate the seed by slicing and putting it under a microscope, hoping to see some tiny images of trees under the lens but everything was to no avail.

To the stranger's eyes, the appearance of leaves was very different from that of the seed. The forms were not consistent with each other and appeared too different to be related. To the stranger's eyes a leaf would be an 'addition' to the seed!

Seeing

To see that the seed, the leaves and fruits of mango are the same thing, we should not LOOK at the differences in their forms of appearance; we should SEE the life that flows through them.

When the seed is put in the right place, in the soil, and the right conditions of moisture and sunlight are present, something will begin to happen inside that dry lifeless object! The energy concealed in its particles will begin to move and rearrange themselves. Then something that was completely hidden to the eye, which *appears* so different from the form of the planted seed, will emerge!

The life in the new fresh stalk is the same one that was in the seed. It is the same life that develops into the trunk and also into leaves and ultimately into the fruit. A thing on that tree would only be an *addition* if it contained a *life* different from the one in the planted seed. So, if an orange fruit grew on a mango tree, that is what would constitute addition. And "addition" not because an orange fruit LOOKS orange and a mango fruit LOOKS green, but because one has the *life* of an orange tree which is different and hence inconsistent with the *life* of a mango tree. Remember that colors of fruits can change (*green* when a mango is unripe and *yellow* when ripe), but life never does!

Life fulfills the Seed

There is nothing that can manifest on a mango tree that was not in the DNA of its seed! A tree may even weigh more than the seed from which it proceeded, but there would still be nothing in the tree – leaves, trunk, branches, fruits, etc. – that was not in the seed! The leaves, the branches, the fruits, and all other *expressions*, are only a fulfillment of what was already hidden in the seed.

Beloved, the written Word is like a seed. When the Spirit of the Word manifests (through revelation or a prophetic fulfillment) carnal eyes will never be able to discern it or find its place in the written Word. Is this not the reason why Jews had waited for their messiah, reciting psalms and words of prophets, but yet could not see the Word when it became flesh. Only a chosen few could testify that "**the Word was made flesh**, *and dwelt among us, (and* **we beheld his glory**, *the glory as of the only begotten of the Father,)* **full of grace and truth**" (Joh.1:14).

Now, if people fail to discern the fulfillment of the written Word, shall they be able to discern what was never written? In Revelation 10:3-4 we read about Seven Thunders uttering things that John was forbidden to write. So, when the time comes for those utterances to be revealed, will their words be an addition to Scripture? Not so. We will be able to recognize and discern the ministry of Thunders by the manifestation of the Life of God's Word. It is that life which will enlighten us to see the Truth of God - "*In him* [the Word] *was life; and* **the life was the light** *of men*" (Joh.1:4).

What to hear and *How* to hear

As with sight, wherein someone can look but not see, so it is with hearing; one may hear something but yet lack understanding. In Mark 4:24 we are warned to "*take heed **what** ye hear*", and in Luke 8:18 to "*take heed … **how** ye hear*". When you are hearing a preacher speaking, do you know **what** you are hearing? And more importantly, **how** are you hearing his words?

It is important to know that the speaking of God through His servants is not the same as that of a highly polished scholar who is careful with putting his nouns, pronouns, and verbs in their right places. Often God has raised uneducated and poor men for the work of ministry. This is expectedly so because carnal reasonings and pride of learned men often hinders them from being led by the Spirit. Concerning Peter and John we read that they were "*unlearned and ignorant*" (Act.4:13). Does this mean that God glorifies ignorance?

Not at all. God can use a learned man, like professor Martin Luther the reformer, just as much as He can use an unlearned man, like William Branham of America. The humility and readiness to be used by the creator is the common attribute in these men.

Talking about William Branham, many people were confounded at his exposition of scriptures. Like one writer put it, William Branham was a paradox in modern history. And as always happens, there were critics, extremists, and also sober believers to his ministry.

Extremists were too overwhelmed with the supernatural signs in Branham's ministry. They elevated his every utterance to have been in-breathed of God so that even a stammer of *"I...I...I...I"* was taken to be the speaking of God. They turned every opinion of brother Branham to be inspired even when he explicitly stated that he was only giving an opinion. This was quite the case when he shared his thoughts on how soon the time of

Gentiles would end. He based his assumption on how quickly seven visions he had seen in 1933 were fulfilling.

William Branham felt that all the seven visions would fulfil by the year 1977. But as a sober preacher who was aware of the fanaticism of setting dates for the return of Christ, he strongly cautioned his congregation against misinterpreting his prediction. He emphasised to his congregation that the prediction wasn't a part of the trance (vision) he had experienced, it was only his opinion:

> Then I turned to look and I seen the United States was a smoldering, something had burned it up, and down beneath there **I said (not in the trance) but I predict**... I predict that these things will take place between now 1933 and 1977...Now, there was seven things spoke of that would happen. Five of them has already happened. There's two left to take place. It'll be that way. **That's in the Name of the Lord it shall be that way**.[5]

What were the people hearing when

---

[5] Conference, 1960.

brother Branham spoke these words? Were they able to distinguish the part which was *"in the Name of the Lord"* from the part which was his opinion? Notice his emphasis on "prediction" in the message *Laodicean Church Age*:

> Now, remember, "predict", **especially you listening at the tape**. I don't say it will be, but predict that it will end by 1977, that the church will go completely into apostasy, and she'll be ousted out of the mouth of God. And the second coming, or the rapture of Christ, might come anytime. **Now, I could miss that a year; I can miss it twenty years, I could miss it a hundred years**. I don't know where. But I just predict that according to a vision He showed me, and taking the time, **the way it's progressing, I say it'll be sometime between '33 and '77** …this great nation is going to strike a war that's going to blow it to bits… And I could be wrong; I'm predicting. Everybody understand say, "amen" if you do.[6]

Did people understand the prophet's words? No! Through time different preachers arose. They took every word, opinion and stammer of William Branham and presented it as THUS SAITH THE LORD. These people were

---

[6] Laodicean Church Age, 1960 (12-11-1960).

so astonished at the great anointing on Branham's ministry. They saw many miracles in his ministry – the dead coming back to life, the blind seeing, squirrels being spoken into existence, people's names and details of their thoughts and activities in life being revealed, and they felt that was God in human flesh! They believed every word he uttered was inspired, and so it followed that 1977 couldn't have been just an opinion but a prophetic utterance. These men spoke as chosen ones to spread the message of Branham to the world. Within circles of the Endtime Message it seemed the closer one was to the prophet the more authentic he was. But let it be known that Judas Iscariot was so close to the Lord Jesus and was even entrusted to be holding the offering bag. Alas, he is the one who killed the Lord!

The Message missionaries from America invested money and other resources into their mission works to Africa, Asia, and other places of the world, believing that they were doing God a service. However, only God knows how much harm and perversion they did to so precious and simple a message William Branham brought. A day of reckoning will surely come. Sadly, gullible people believed the ministers but much to the disappointment of some who noticed that the alleged 'prophecies' did not fulfil.

One day I was watching a video of a man who had been a believer in the message of William Branham for over 30 years but later rejected it. "William Branham was wrong! His 1977 prophecy never fulfilled!" he said. What stupidity! You spend years creating a high tower of 'Truth'; you close your ears to people calling out to tell you that you are misrepresenting a man's message, and when you realise the 'Error', you start dismantling it with great relish whilst blaming the man that you misunderstood! Unfortunately, so loud were the preachings and teachings of Message preachers from America that they deafened the actual voice and teachings of William Branham. As though all this is not injustice enough to the prophet, many modern denominational preachers now sieve the little information they know about Branham through the mess they see in the Mess-Age!

"Mystery" or "Mysteries"?

Some people have a one-track mind. Such a mind can only hear and understand words in their immediate or primary context. So, if William Branham explains about how the seventh church age messenger will reveal "all mysteries according to Revelation 10:7", they will check what the verse in the Bible actually says, see the difference, and reject everything else William Branham is speaking. On other end of the spectrum are extremists who exalt Branham above Scripture and choose to quote Revelation 10:7 according to how Branham phrased it, not according to how the verse is actually stated in the Bible. Both these attitudes are results of not having ears to hear what the Spirit speaks.

It is important to note that when God gives a revelation to a preacher, the man will use his illustrations, examples, and various words to express the Truth of the Word he has received. The expressions and words may be so many but the revelation itself may only fit in three or four sentences.

That is what happened to William Branham when he was teaching on the Seven Seals. The actual inspiration (revelation) he received on each seal can only be found in one or two paragraphs. But each revelation was accompanied by so many words of explanation. Now, the words **point to** the Truth of the revelation, but the truth itself is not in the words. Actually, the words of explanations may even contain wrong examples, wrong scripture quotations, etcetera. But the LIFE or THOUGHT behind the words will never be inconsistent if it is a true revelation!

Now, when quoting a verse, a preacher may use its primary meaning to teach something. However, a part of the same verse can be used as a *synecdoche* to illustrate something else other than the primary context of the verse. We see God using this method on His own words in Scripture. Hosea 11:1 is an example. In this verse God speaks about how He delivered Israel from Egypt – *"When Israel was a child, then I loved him, and called my son out of Egypt"*. In the book of Matthew we read that this verse was fulfilled in an event that occurred in the life of Jesus when he was a baby - *"he took the young child and his mother by night, and departed into Egypt: and he was there until the death of Herod that it might be fulfilled which was spoken of the Lord by the prophet, saying, Out of Egypt have I called my son"*(Mat.2:14).

Someone may argue that this explanation may license people to misapply scriptures. Well, *"the natural man receiveth not the things of the Spirit of God: for they are foolishness unto him: neither can he know them, because they are spiritually discerned"* (1 Cor.2:14). When the wise and spiritual hear a man speak, they will discern the truth and consistency of the thought being expounded, and will know how a message can be 100% correct when heard and looked at in its proper context, and yet again 100% wrong when stretched beyond the thought it is intended to convey.

Prophets are human beings!

When the anointing is on a prophet and he speaks THUS SAITH THE LORD, that is God speaking. However, that Spirit is not always on a prophet and that is where trouble begins for many people – failing to distinguish the prophet as a human being from being a messenger of God. When John the Baptist proclaimed, *"Behold the Lamb of God, which taketh away the sin of the world"* (Joh.1:29), that was inspiration and the anointing on him. Later on when he was imprisoned, and sent his disciples to go and ask Jesus, "*Art thou he that should come? or look we for another?*" (Luk.7:19), that was a man speaking. Sons and daughters of God are able to discern when God is speaking because they are born and are led of the Spirit (Rom.8:14).

It's an old spirit!

We don't get discouraged at hearing the misinformation and deception which has gone around the world because we know that all this is not a new occurrence, it is an old spirit.

Do you remember when the Lord said to the disciples that some of them would not die until they saw the kingdom of God come with power? (Mar.9:1). Some critics of the Bible point to that verse and say, "All disciples of Christ died and to this day Jesus hasn't yet come back to earth to establish His kingdom!" When these critics hear the words of the Lord in Mark 9:1, do they know *what* the Lord Jesus was speaking about? No, they cannot know because they don't know *how* to hear!

Again, do you remember the time when the Lord said if He desired, John would be alive till He came? Well, news (and perhaps a teaching) went out that John would never die! *"Jesus saith unto him, If I will that he tarry till I come, what is that to thee? follow thou me. Then went this saying abroad among the brethren, that that disciple should not die: yet Jesus said not unto him, He shall not die; but, If I will that he tarry till I come, what is that to thee? This is the disciple which testifieth of these things, and wrote these things: and we know that his testimony is true"*.

To all who have received and perceived the revelation of God's Word in this end-time, *"Blessed are your eyes, for they see: and your ears, for they hear"* (Mat.13:16).

6.

In the Name of Jesus...

*"Lo, I am with you always, even unto the
end of the world"*

Mat.28:20

One great promise of Christ to us is His presence. Apart from enabling us to see the revelation of His Word, His presence also gives us power over evil spirits. When He sends us to pray for a person afflicted with an evil spirit or an illness, we can boldly cast it out *"in the name of Jesus!"*

Now, before I continue testifying about the power of the name of Jesus, let me take this space to address a fallacy that has confused some believers. The false doctrine states that prayer can only be effective when we use the correct Hebrew pronunciation of *Yeshua.* This doctrine is influencing some circles of believers in India. Many have gone into vain jangling striving over letters and words of scripture, but understanding neither what they believe or teach to others!

Unknown to many *Endtime Message* believers, this is not a new teaching or 'revelation'. The doctrine started in the 1930s within the Church of God movement. The cause of the false doctrine is the same problem of hanging on letters and failing to discern the *life* of the Word.

Addressing the *Yeshua* doctrine

Advocates of the Yeshua doctrine argue that because a name of a person is a *proper noun*[7] it cannot change when spoken in another language. So, although the New Testament was written in Greek and the Messiah's name was in Hebrew, it has to be written and pronounced in Hebrew. It is further argued that the letter "J", or the sound it represents, never existed at the time of the Lord, and so no one could have called Him by the pronunciation with a "J" sound. Extremists further claim that *Iesous*, the Greek rendition of the name *Yeshua,* from which the English word *Jesus* was derived, is a compound word consisting of names of pagan gods – *IEU* and *SUS* (Zeus). Here

---

[7] A *proper noun* (also called *proper name*) is a particular name of a person, thing, or place. For example, "James", "London", etc.

a conspiracy theory is at play to suggest an evil scheme by Bible translators. And talking about conspiracy theories, the Internet is so full of them. Unfortunately, many Christians (including preachers) get whatever they find exciting on the *World Wide Web*, without carrying an objective analysis of facts.

A simple study on challenges of translation shows various difficulties that are often encountered when translating proper nouns from one language to another. The translation process of the Bible from Hebrew and Greek into English presents a typical example of this.

Challenges of translation

First, is it true that a proper noun should always be translated unchanged into another language? And, did Bible translators really conspire to make people worship pagan gods when they translated Yeshua to Iesous or to Jesus? This is simply not true. Advocates of this doctrine are rather too sanguine and quick at rubbishing work which is a result of many years of pain-staking scholarly efforts.

The work of translating scriptures was not an easy undertaking. Like other works of linguistics, there were challenges of translating names.

Translation & Transliteration

There is *translation* and *transliteration*. The aim of translation is to 'transfer' the meaning of words from one language to another. Here a challenge rises when there is an objective to let words be pronounced correctly in the target language. This is achieved by transliteration.

Transliteration involves changing letters of a word in one language into letters of the alphabet of the target language in order to preserve its pronunciation. This may seem a simple process when dealing with sentences but problematic when you encounter *proper nouns*.

Proper nouns are words used to

refer to a particular thing. They are different from general names of places or things. For example, "person" is a general term but "Peter" is specific and hence is called a proper noun (or *proper name*).

There are different strategies used by scholars to translate proper nouns. One strategy regards names as labels for persons or objects. This strategy requires a proper name to be copied exactly as it is into the target text. Another strategy considers the need to preserve pronunciation and hence asserts that proper names "can be transcribed or transliterated or adapted on the level of spelling [and] phonology."[8]

There is yet another strategy which requires translating the meaning of words so that a person named "Blessing" in English will be called "Daliso" in Nyanja, a Zambian

---

[8] Franco Aixela cited by Rouholla Zarei [Online] in the article *Proper Nouns in Translation: Should they be Translated.* Available online: http://ler.letras.up.pt/uploads/ficheiros/4666.pdf [Accessed: 15th November, 2016].

language. This allows preserving the meaning of a name in the target language. But as you can see in this example, the pronunciation of a name in the original language is lost.

How "*Yeshua*" became "*Jesus*"

In the light of what has been explained, it is important to know that Yeshua was *transliterated* as Iesous in Greek to preserve its pronunciation. But when further translated into English a completely different pronunciation came up. How did this happen? Was it a conspiracy? Not so. Let us look at the explanation in the following sequence:

1. The name *Yeshua* is a Hebrew transliteration which begins with the sound of "**Y**" as in the word "**Y**es"

Note: The New Testament was written in Greek. In this language the "**Y**" sound is represented by the letter "*I*". So, in order to convey the same pronunciation in Greek, *Yeshua* had to be transliterated starting with the letter *I* and hence the name *Iesous.*

2. In the name *Yeshua,* after the "Y" sound comes the "*e*" sound, as in "Y*es.*" There was no problem in transliterating this sound as there was an equivalent letter in Greek to represent it, *Iesous.*

Note: The "*e*" in *Yeshua* is pronounced as in the word "Y*es*", not as in "S*ee*". However, when the name was transliterated into Iesous and then into Jesus, English speakers pronounced the "*e*" as in "S*ee*" and hence the modern mispronunciation of Jesus. Even so, a number of languages have retained the correct pronunciation of the name.

3. Next we come to the "*sh*" sound in *Yeshua* This is where translators encountered a problem because whilst this sound exists in Hebrew it does not exist in Greek. So, translators went for the letter in the Greek alphabet which is close to the "*sh*" sound and that was the *sigma* which gives an "*s*" sound

as in "*Sad*."

<u>Note</u>: If the English Bible translators had transliterated the name Jesus straight from Hebrew, the name would have maintained the "*sh*" sound found in Ye*sh*ua because English language has the "*sh*" sound. But they transliterated Jesus from the Greek Iesous and hence the disappearance of the "*sh*" sound in English.

4. The "*u*" sound in Yesh*u*a is the same as in "r*u*le" or "tr*u*e".

<u>Note</u>: The English language provides two ways of pronouncing the sound of letter "*u*". It can be pronounced as in the word "tr*u*e" or as in the word "c*u*t". In Ieso*u*s it is correctly pronounced with the "*u*" sound as in "tr*u*e". But English speakers mispronounced it as in the word "c*u*t."

5. The "*a*" sound at the end of Yeshu*a* is replaced with the "*s*" in Iesou*s*.

<u>Note</u>: The Greek language has genders

for nouns so that all names that end with the letter *s* are male names. It is for this reason that although Iesous was an attempt to transliterate the name Yeshua, it never ended with an *u* sound (as in the word tr*u*e) but with *s* to denote its masculinity. An example of this in the Scripture is how the Hebrew name *Isaiah* appears as *Esias* in the New Testament (Luk.4:17). Note that the New Testament was written in Greek.

6. When translating Iesous into English, the "**Y**" sound of "**I**" (as in Y*es*) was at first retained but later was lost to the "**J**" sound as in *Jam*.

<u>Note</u>: Letter *J* at one time was just another style or shape for writing letter *I*. In Roman numerals it was used to show the end of a series of *Is*. For example, number *13* when written as a Roman numeral is *XIII* but would be written with the last *I* having a serif tail, *XIIJ*.

In the alphabet the two letters "I" and "J" were also used interchangeably and were both pronounced with the "Y" sound as in "Yes" so that a Hebrew name with the "Y" sound like *Yeshua* became *Iesous* in Greek or *Iesus* in English. This can be seen in the Tyndale version of the Bible, known to have been the first English translation. A verse in this Bible reads: *"She had brought forth hir first sonne and called hys name Iesus"* (Mat.1:25).

In later English versions of the Bible names starting with the *Y*-sound were transliterated with letter *J* because then it had the *Y*-sound. So words such as *Yerushalaim* and *Yarden* became transliterated as *Jerusalem* and *Jordan* respectively.

It was in the year 1524 when an Italian scholar, Gian Trissino (1478–1550), distinguished the two letters to represent two different sounds so that *J* now had the *'dg'* sound as in the word *"Jam*. However, the English language Bibles were never updated to take into account the new sound of J. Gradually the *Y*-sound was lost to the new *J-*

sound. Over the decades and a century people became used with reading and pronouncing "*J*" as in "*J*am" . Thus, words like *Jerusalem* and *Iesus* were now pronounced with the '*dg*' sound as we know them today. In the year 1611 a new version of the Bible, the King James Version, had the objective of acknowledging the vulgar (common) pronunciation of words. The purpose of this was to use words in Scripture that people were familiar with. As noted in the *Britannica Encyclopaedia*:

> An elaborate set of rules was contrived to curb individual proclivities and to ensure the translation's scholarly and nonpartisan character. In contrast to earlier practice, the new version was to use vulgar forms of proper names (e.g., "Jonas" or "Jonah" for the Hebrew "Yonah").[9]

Enough with theological explanations, the question which arises now is, does it matter to God if we use the Hebrew pronunciation of Yeshua, or the modern

---

[9] Britannica Encyclopaedia (2016). *King James Version Sacred Text.*[Online] Available from:
https://www.britannica.com/topic/King-James-Version
[Accessed 17th November, 2016].

English term of Jesus? A few testimonies may help us understand the answer to this question.

Testimony of John Mark Louse

In a remote region of Uganda called Karamoja lived a man called John Mark Louse. His testimony has gone around the world. Although poor, uneducated, and living in a region cut from modern civilisation, he experienced a vision of the Lord Jesus and was commissioned to take the Gospel to the natives of the region. The following is a narration of the testimony by brother John Mark:

●●●

Suddenly, a light appeared in the hut and immediately the wind and the quaking stopped. The nature of this light was unique, it had a bluish brightness. All these happenings were too much for me, and I wanted to run away but I was paralyzed. My joints were weakened; they refused to respond to my command to take off. My strength was gone.

In the light, the Lord Jesus Christ appeared. He looked directly at me with a lovely smiling face. He pointed at me and said, *"My servant, you have been highly favored, your purpose of being here in Teso is two-fold. You have been brought here because of salvation and secondly, you have a ministry; you are my apostle and my appearing to you is to give you this ministry."*

During this time, as the Lord was talking, I had a question deep inside my heart and the question was, *"How will I preach the Word of God as an apostle since I am not educated?"* I did not utter it out. But the Lord again pointed at me and said, *"I know why you doubt, I am going to give you the ability to understand English to minister my Word. You will be able to speak, read and write for I have chosen you to be a light to your people. You are going to begin this ministry here in Teso, and you will continue with it even up to Karamoja and other lands. You will also fly in planes to other countries to minister my Word."*

●●●

God not only gave John Mark salvation but the ability to read and understand English. God also revealed to him the truth about Bible doctrines. An interesting account of this was when he was puzzled about the *original sin* that occurred in the garden of Eden and the incident of *"sons of God"* marrying *"daughters of men"* in Genesis chapter 6.

●●●

There were two places in the Bible that I didn't understand. The first one was Genesis chapter 3 where it talks about the eating of the fruit of the tree of knowledge of good and evil, and the second one was Genesis chapter 6. These were very disturbing scriptures to me then and it compelled me to approach the pastor… to explain to me the meaning of these two passages of Scriptures.

The pastor explained to me that the fruit of the

forbidden tree in Genesis 3 was a natural fruit but it was forbidden to be eaten. He told me that Genesis 6 was about the heavenly angels who married the earthly daughters of men and begat children who were known as "*giants*". But I told him that in Matthew, Jesus said that in the resurrection there will be no marriage because people will be like angels who don't marry. Then the man told me that, with the Bible you don't have to read it and put all your heart into it, otherwise you will become mad. So, because of this, it led me into seeking God about what he said and the Lord answered me in my prayer that, *"those Pentecostal elders don't have the answer to those scriptures you are asking. Wait, in the near future you will get the answer to those scriptures because there was a man I have used and the answer is within his books and that man, I have already taken him."*

…One evening, as I was seated at the public garden with the friend whom I stayed with at his home, conversing and reading our Bibles, a student of the *Soroti Flying School* came to join us. He came from Kenya and was also a Pentecostal Christian. He related to us several testimonies of the mighty men of God, like Billy Graham, Oral Roberts, T. L. Osborn. Then he talked about William Marrion Branham. He told us that Branham was a prophet and that God used him mightily. I asked him, "Do you have some of his books?" He replied, "Yes, I have some of them in my room." And I requested him to go and bring them to us since the place was near. He gladly agreed and went and brought us some few copies.

After we had read those books, both of us were totally convinced that this man was a prophet of God and the two questions that I had about Genesis 3 and 6 were answered in one of the books. From that I was fully convinced that this was the Elijah who was promised to come.

The whole church in Soroti believed the Message and believers were baptized by immersion in the Name of the Lord Jesus Christ according to the Scriptures.[10]

●●●

I forever cherish the memories of the few times I spent with this gallant servant of God. When I invited him to Zambia, after preaching during one service, a prayer line of sick people formed. Next to be prayed for was a young lady who could hardly walk. Her legs were swollen and she was having a hard time to breathe. She had a damaged liver.

"In the Name of the Lord Jesus Christ receive your healing!" brother John Mark prayed. There wasn't any drama to his prayers. He prayed soberly but with authority. The following day we were amazed to see the girl healed. It is now about two years when this testimony occurred, and the girl is still healed.

---

[10] Read the full testimony of John Mark Louse on this link: http://www.propheticrevelation.net/richard_gan/johnmarklo use.htm

So, what healed the girl? Was it the shouting or pronunciation of the name Jesus? Not so! If it were so why didn't the mentioning of the name of Jesus not work for the sons of Sceva? And why doesn't the mentioning of the name not work for many people who often shout and command various blessings in the name of Jesus?

Sons of Sceva

In the book of Acts we read about a group of young men who saw apostle Paul casting out demons and they started imitating his ministry. They started a 'deliverance ministry' and were using the Jesus-Name formula to pray for people. (Isn't this typical of many young people today who have enthused themselves into starting ministries which the Lord has not commissioned?).

The sons of Sceva began to pray over people "in the name of Jesus". One day things didn't go well when an evil spirit spoke from a man asking, *"Jesus I know, and Paul I know; but who are ye?"* (Act.19:15).

Now, what pronunciation did this demon use when speaking the name "Jesus"? Well, whatever it was, whether in Hebrew as *Yeshua* or in Greek as *Iesous*, one thing should be certain: the demon was not afraid to speak the name! That tells you and I that the power of the name of the Lord does not lie in speaking or mentioning it as is commonly believed among many Christians. However, there was something different when Paul mentioned *"in the name of Jesus."* Demons trembled. So, what was the difference?

The difference was that when Paul addressed the demons by saying, "I command you, in the name of the Lord Jesus, to come out of the man", he truly was speaking in the name of the Lord. God sent him and His presence accompanied him and that was what evil spirits feared. To do things in the name of the Lord is to perform them in accordance with His will and power.

When you pray to God, He does not sit still waiting to hear if your vowels and consonants are coming out right. What God is able to do when we pray is not a question of whether we pronounce the name of Jesus Christ correctly but whether we have the power of Christ inside our hearts – "*Now unto **Him that is able** to do exceeding abundantly above all that we ask or think, **according to the power that worketh in us**" (Eph. 3:20).

The power in us is the power of faith that the Spirit of God gives us. It is not a physical power that expresses itself in our loud shouting when we pray. One person may pray quietly and another loudly but what will make the difference is the presence of God.

A personal testimony

There was a call to go and pray for someone. Together with a deacon we went to the house where the patient was. When we entered the living room we told everyone who was there to leave us with the patient (we did not want other people's unbelief to interfere with our faith). Strangely, just as soon as I started whispering some words to the Lord in prayer, we heard a person screaming so terribly. Next the door banged opened, and here was an old woman manifesting demons and three people were struggling to hold and prevent her from entering the room where we were. She came scrolling on the floor like a snake until she lay prostrate where we were standing. The family was terrified and didn't know what was happening to the elderly woman. Well, we had not shouted any prayers but the demons in the woman had already felt the presence of the power of God.

That's what really matters, the presence of the owner of the name. Unfortunately, the Yeshua *"wind of doctrine"* has deceived people into *"doting about questions and strifes of words, whereof cometh envy, strife* [and] *railings"* (Eph.4:14, 1 Tim.6:4). Such people are trying to make the

Gospel of Christ become complex as though it is Greek and Hebrew lexicons that will save them. Surely the 'fear of Paul' has befallen them as they have moved away from the simplicity that is in Christ – "*But I fear, lest by any means, as the serpent beguiled Eve through his subtlety, so your minds should be corrupted from the simplicity that is in Christ.*" (2 Cor.11:3).

Looking at the lateness of the hour we are living in, we do not have the luxury of time to entertain being "*tossed to and fro, and carried about with every wind of doctrine*" (Eph. 4:14). It is simply too late to go into "*vain jangling*" (1 Tim. 1:6).

7.

Finding fault

"But I say unto you, That every idle word that men shall speak, they shall give account thereof in the day of judgment"

Mat. 12:36

In 1963 a most remarkable event occurred when William Branham received the revelation of the Seven Seals of Revelation chapter 6. That was perhaps the greatest supernatural event of the twentieth century. What William Branham taught on the subject had never been heard before. No, the teaching he gave was not a presentation of findings of a research or a thesis. It was a heaven-sent revelation regarding what the Seals meant.

Two things are most remembered about the Seals event.

First, it was preceded by a prophetic vision which brother Branham had narrated on 30th December, 1962 in a message titled, *Is this the Sign of the End, Sirs?*[11]In this vision brother Branham talked about hearing a blast which was followed by an appearance of angels.

Second, the blast and visit of angels were strikingly soon fulfilled when brother Branham was caught up in a

---

[11] Find sermon here - http://branham.org/messageaudio/62-1230E

constellation of seven angels. The angels formed a spectacular visible appearance in the sky which got photographed and appeared on the cover of *Science Magazine* on 19th April 1963, in *Life Magazine* on 17th May 1963, and in the London Observer. The *Encyclopaedia Britannica* also recorded details of this cloud in their 1965 year book.

Mystery Cloud photographed in Arizona, 1963

When scientific data about the cloud

was collected and analysed, the phenomenon remained a mystery! The cloud was about 50 miles long, 30 miles wide and 26 miles high. Scientists stated that at 26 miles high it is impossible for a cloud to form because it is outside the earth's atmosphere. Further investigations indicated that there were no rockets, high flying aircraft or space equipment operating in the area at that time, to form such a Cloud.

While the cloud remained a mystery to everyone, those who had heard details about its prophecy in 1962 knew what had happened.

The seven angels instructed William Branham to go to Jeffersonville Indiana where he would receive the revelation of the Seals. The rest is now history and we know the profound revelation that was given to believers.

However, as always happens, 'Pharisees', 'Teachers of the Law', and 'false witnesses', rose to refute, argue, and falsify facts about the testimony of the mystery cloud and the teaching of

Seven Seals which followed, but yet understanding neither what they say, nor whereof they affirm (1 Tim.1:7).

Criticism against the revelation of the Seven Seals

The critics have said, there was nothing new to what Branham taught on the Seals. He has been accused to have actually repeated word for word what a Baptist theologian, Dr. Clarence Larkin, had already written some forty years earlier in his work, *The Book of Revelation*.

One critic (said to have once been a follower of Branham's ministry) during a convention at which I was the speaker in India boldly and emotionally argued against William Branham's claim of having supernaturally received the inspiration on the teaching of the Seals. According to him, William Branham plagiarized Clarence Larkin's work.

Upon hearing the man's misplaced and flawed arguments my greater surprise lay not in what he was saying, but how such an uninformed minister had risen to high ranks of being looked upon as a minister of the Gospel by many in the *Endtime Message*. The man proclaimed:

> Everything that's been written by Clarence Larkin in this book [*pointing to Larkin's book*] is in the Seven Seals book [*of William Branham*]. Check it! What is this? Is that revelation from the seven angels?

Is this true? Was the zeal of this man in congruence with facts? Let us look into what Branham and Larkin both said and see how emphasis, emotion, and zeal does not always amount to someone knowing what they are talking about.

What says the facts?

We will now proceed to examine facts surrounding the plagiarism accusation.

May I first emphasise that in prophetic

study, it is more important to compare teachings on the basis of *when* foretold events would occur than *what* the symbols that constitute a prophecy mean.

The interpretation of symbols is often common or similar across different denominations, and perhaps other religions. So, there is nothing special when two people both say a *sword* means war, or *red* means bloodshed. This is well illustrated in the difference between what Larkin and Branham taught on the Seals.

First Seal

Here is what the Scripture says about the First Seal: *"And I saw, and behold a white horse: and he that sat on him had a bow; and a crown was given unto him: and he went forth conquering, and to conquer"* (Rev. 6:1-2).

Concerning who the white-horse rider is Larkin wrote:

Who is the 'Rider' upon this White Horse? He is not Christ, as some claim, for Christ, as the LAMB, is holding the 'Seven Sealed Book' and breaking its

'Seals.' Christ does not appear as a White Horse Rider until chapter 19:11-16, when He comes with the armies of Heaven to engage in the Battle of Armageddon… this White Horse Rider is the ANTICHRIST…

This 'Rider' has a 'bow', no arrow is mentioned, and he is not crowned at first, but a crown will be given to him later, the 'Stephanos' or 'Victor's Crown,' as a reward for his victories which are prolonged and bloodless.

Surely, reading Larkin's words up to this far shows a striking similarity with the words Branham used in his preaching on the Seals. Ofcourse Larkin's book must have been on the list he read when he mentioned in his First Seal sermon that he studied different books on the subject - "I have read every book on it I could find….I got Smith's book on Daniel , of revelations…and others, I read two or three".[12] However, when you read on what Larkin explains on the First and the rest of the Seals, what you see are totally different interpretations.

Notice how Larkin placed emphasis

---

[12] The First Seal, page 139.Paragraph 265.

on the white-horse rider being a person who was yet to rise in the future:

> This 'White Horse Rider' will be Satan's 'SUPERMAN.' The Scriptures clearly teach that there is some day to arise a human being who shall be the embodiment of all Satanic power. He will be known as the 'WILFUL KING' because he shall do according to his own will.

Although William Branham used Larkin's words to describe the white-horse rider as an "Antichrist" and "Superman", he emphasised that the rider was not a person but a spirit of Nicolaitanism which began to influence the early church: [13]

> *A white horse rider went out.* See? Who is he? He is mighty in his conquering power. He is a great power in his conquering power. You want me to tell you who he is? He is the antichrist....When he starts off, as a Nicolaitane spirit in the church he is a spirit. You can't crown a spirit. But three hundred years later, he become a pope, and then they crowned him. He had no crown , to start with. But he got a crown, later, see, when that spirit become incarnate …Nicolaitane doctrine become a man,

---

[13] Note that although Clarence Larkin when teaching about Revelation Chapter 2 and 3 taught about the deeds of the Nicolaitane in the first church age, a thing William Branham read and also taught, he did not take that as the interpretation of the First Seal.

then they could crown him.[14]

And what did Larkin and Branham say about when the white-horse rider would be crowned? Larkin explained that it would be fulfilled at the beginning of Daniel's Seventieth week, when the antichrist will be made "head of the Ten Federated Kingdoms of the revived Roman Empire." Here are his words:

> This is the picture of a brilliant, strategical, and irresistible conqueror, whose victories will dazzle the world, and elevate him to a leadership that will place him at the Head of the Ten Federated Kingdoms of the revived Roman Empire. As a subaltern, like Napoleon I, he will rise from the ranks until a crown will be given him. His triumphs will be due to his skilful diplomacy….In other words this White Horse Rider is the ANTICHRIST. He is the "PRINCE WHO IS TO COME" of Daniel's Vision of the "Seventy Weeks," and who will confirm the Covenant for "ONE WEEK," the last or "Seventieth Week," with Daniel's people the Jews. Dan. 9:27.

Is this what William Branham taught? Did he say that the crowning of the white horse rider is yet to be fulfilled when political leaders of Europe will

---

[14] The First Seal, Paragraph 295 – 301.

give power to the antichrist, before the Week of Daniel?

First William Branham does not point to the future, to the beginning of the Seventieth Week of Daniel, as the time when the white horse rider will be crowned. He taught that the crowning already occurred when the papacy was established in the fourth century. He said:

> He had no crown, to start with, but a crown was given him. Notice later he was given a crown…that was three hundred years later, at the Nicaea Council…When he started out, a spirit of Nicolaitane, to form an organisation among the people. And then it kept going on, going on, going on, become 'a saying', then it become 'a doctrine.'[15]

Now, what manner of conquering will the white-horse rider accomplish?

Clarence Larkin wrote that his triumphs will be due to his skilful diplomacy. He saw this person's conquering as a political and diplomatic accomplishment. What brother

---

[15] First Seal, Paragraph 297.

Branham said about the conquering is quite different. He explained that the conquering referred to a religious doctrine that enabled the clergy to rule over people instead of the Holy Spirit. Again he pointed back to the early stages of church history as a point when this practice began. In his interpretation there is no reference to the conquering being a diplomatic strategy of the Antichrist or that it will take place around the time of the Seventieth Week. Here is what he said:

> Remember, in the church ages…the Holy Spirit was against a certain thing they got started in that church age, and that was called 'the deeds of the Nicolaitanes'… *Nikao* means 'to conquer'. *Laity* means 'the church', the laity. Nico-laitane, 'to conquer the laity.' Take the Holy Spirit out of the church and give it all to one holy man.[16]

Let us move on to the Second Seal.

Second Seal

At the convention in India the anti-Branham preacher produced a

---

[16] First Seal, Paragraph 295.

document with two columns. In one column were Larkin's words and in the next Branham's words. He highlighted words that were similar and concluded that Branham copied his teaching from Larkin. Here is an excerpt of the table.

1920 Clarence Larkin	1963 William Branham
The symbolism is very clear. Red, the colour of the Horse, is a symbol of BLOOD, and the **Sword is a symbol of WAR.**	Now, here's my revelation of it: This is Satan again… But you find out here that this man has a **sword so he pertains to church political war.**

Talk of ignorance and deceptive presumption? The man quoted isolated words and hid entire explanations given by Larkin and Branham. Here is the entire explanation of what Larkin wrote about the Second Seal:

> There is no need to tarry long with this SEAL. When it was broken John heard the second, or 'Calf-like Living Creature' say, 'Come,' and a 'RED HORSE' appeared and went forth, whose Rider was given a 'GREAT SWORD,' and who had power to take peace from the earth, and cause men to kill one another. The symbolism is very clear. Red, the color of the Horse, is a symbol of BLOOD, and the Sword is a symbol of WAR.

The time is clearly that prophesied by Christ—'*And ye shall hear of wars and rumors of wars . . . for nation shall rise against nation, and kingdom against kingdom.*' Matt. 24:6-7. This seems to imply that the Antichrist will not have everything his own way, and that his Autocratic methods will lead to insubordination and civil wars among the nations under some great leader represented by the Rider of the Red Horse, whose 'Great Sword' is symbolical of the awful destruction of human life that will follow. This is a fulfilment of 1. Thess. 5:3. '*When they shall say PEACE and SAFETY; then sudden destruction cometh upon them, as travail upon a woman with child; and they shall not escape.*' We learn from this 'Seal' that wars are likely to break out at any time and that there will be no peace on the earth until the return of the 'Prince of Peace.'

As many who have read Branham's teaching on the Second Seal are aware, what Branham taught is way different from what you read in Larkin's words.

About the Second Seal Revelation 6:3-4 reads: *"And when he had opened the second seal, I heard the second beast say, Come and see. And there went out another horse that was red: and power was given to him that sat thereon to take peace from the earth, and that they should kill one another: and there was given unto him a great sword."*

As was stated at the beginning, it is ridiculous to raise a case of plagiarism simply because both Branham and Larkin interpret "sword" and "red" to mean *war* and *bloodshed* respectively. Those are common symbols in prophetic Bible study. This is evident by what Jehovah Witnesses, Adventists, and many others have explained about the Second Seal and other similar biblical prophecies. Like stated earlier, in prophetic study, it is more important to compare teachings on the basis of *when* foretold events would occur than *what* the symbols that constitute a prophecy mean. Otherwise we will have to say Adventists, Catholics, and Pentecostals all believe the same thing. Thus, to get a complete picture of what Larkin and Branham said about the Second Seal, and how similar or different their teachings are, we should compare the following two things: What kind of war is the Second Seal about, and most importantly, in what time-span would it fulfil?

As shown in Larkin's words above, his interpretation referred to *"insubordination and civil wars among the nations under some great leader represented by the Rider of the Red Horse."* In Larkin's interpretation the fulfilment of the Second Seal is future oriented. Even so, about how long these wars will go on, he left it open ended until the coming of Christ, the Prince of Peace - *"We learn from this 'Seal' that wars are likely to break out at any time and that there will be no peace on the earth until the return of the 'Prince of Peace.' "*

Let us now look at what William Branham taught on the Second Seal.

'A red horse; and his rider goes forth, power given to him to slay with a great sword.' Now here is my revelation of it. This is Satan, again. It's the devil, again, in another form…. Notice the change of color of these horses…The same system riding on another color, power, from the innocent white to a bloody red… Now listen. I'm quoting from the martyrology, 'From the time of_of Saint Augustine of Hippo, until 1586,' on the Roman martyrology, 'the Roman Catholic church put sixty-eight million Protestants to death.' Was his sword red? Was he riding a red horse? What was it? The same power; the same rider. There is the Seal. They admit, 'sixty-eight million,' on the martyrology, besides all those put to death outside of that. Oh, mercy! During the dark ages, there were millions fed to lions, and slaughtered in every way, because they wouldn't bow down to that Catholic dogma.

In these words of brother Branham we notice two things. First, the war he mentions is a religious-political war by the Catholic system against what they perceived to be heretics. Second, this seal was already fulfilled during the Dark Ages when many people were killed by the Catholic system. It is important to note here that brother Branham's interpretation has a specific time-context of the Dark Ages. His interpretation also tells a related story of events through the Seven Seals:

> His bow had no arrows, at first, but his 'great sword' did. He done his killing, later, and changed from white horse to red horse; the same, exactly, devil, with his sword.

Space does not allow me to go through all the Seven Seals. However, this topic would not be complete without looking at the interesting case of the Third Seal. Details of the vision John saw concerning this seal can be found in

Revelation 6:5-6.

Third Seal

Larkin takes the "**famine**" of the Third Seal as a literal depravation of food that is yet to fulfil during a time of distress and war in the world. He also calls the Third Seal's horse rider as the "**preserver of food.**" Branham, on the other hand said this rider was the same Antichrist spirit that rode the first horse in the First Seal. He pointed the fulfilment of the Third Seal not to the future but back to the Dark Ages as a period of spiritual famine when the true Word of Life was deprived from people as they got subjected to religious dogma and superstition. And what about the statement *"See thou hurt not the oil and the wine"* in the Third Seal? Larkin took these words and again looked into the future for some war and famine which will one day occur. He wrote:

> What is meant by not hurting the oil and wine, may be, that as the Olive tree and grapevine do not bear their fruit until some months after the wheat and barley harvest, and grow without much attention,

their crops would not be so much affected by war, and therefore the Olive trees and grapevines were not to be ruthlessly destroyed by invaders for they were needed for medicinal purposes.

This is not what Branham said about the *"oil"* and *"wine"*! Again, he pointed us back to historical events of the Dark Ages explaining that the oil spoke of the "anointing" and the wine as "the stimulation of revelation" upon the few elect whom God had protected from the religious traditions and falsehoods of that time.

Surely, in the light of these diametrically opposed interpretations, for someone to pull isolated similar words or statements and conclude that Branham plagiarised Larkin's teaching on Seals, would not just be a matter of misconstruing facts but more a case of deception. But this is not strange. Since time immemorial, whenever God raises a ministry, there has always been a Dathan and Kora to contend against a a true prophetic ministry, a Hananiah drawing people's attention from a 'judgmental' Jeremiah to a false hope of prosperity and joy. There has always been a Judas to betray Jesus. And yes, there has also always been a Jannes and Jambres to withstand the true miracles and truth of God – *"As Jannes and Jambres withstood Moses, so do these also resist the truth: men of corrupt minds, reprobate concerning the faith"* (2 Tim.3:8).

Resisting the truth of the 1963 Mystery Cloud

Julian Assange says, *"There are conspiracies everywhere. There are also crazed conspiracy theories. It's important not to confuse these two. Generally, when there's enough facts about a conspiracy we simply call this news."*

How many facts or witnesses are required for a 'conspiracy' or alleged lie to graduate into 'news' or truth? Two witnesses? Three witnesses? Well, the resurrected Christ was witnessed by over 500 people. Was this number enough for a critic like Porphyry, a roman philosopher, who had made up his mind to criticize Christianity regardless of the evidence? No.

Many Bible critics don't believe in the stories of miracles in the ministry of Jesus Christ. Others even go to extents of denying the very idea that there was once a person called Jesus. They dismiss accounts of the Gospels to be false. Well, that is not worse. A number of conspiracy theorists today deny the Jewish holocaust which occurred less than a century ago! A fool will go on the Internet and read some 'interesting' stuff by an anti-Semitic blogger. He or she will believe whatever tommyrot is presented about why the holocaust was a hoax. This would be despite all the unassailable evidence of events surrounding the Shoah.

Looking at such bizarre disbelief, would it be too strange to have critics who try to dig into dates William Branham mentioned about the Cloud in an effort to try to discredit his testimony? Well, we know what we have seen and experienced. Our testimony is not based on some picture brother Branham testified to us. Rather

God appeared to us and opened our eyes to see the Truth in the man's ministry. Like Peter of old we can boldly testify that *"we have not followed cunningly devised fables, when we made known unto you the power and coming of our Lord Jesus Christ, but were eyewitnesses of his majesty"* (2 Pet.1:16). The workings and testimonies of God are not established by some social scientist or journalist going round to gather data. Until that divine voice reaches the heart, one cannot discern the Truth of God.

A number of anti-Branham preachers who have risen to argue against the Mystery Cloud testimony have little, prejudiced, or no correct understanding of William Branham's ministry. The issue of the Branham-Larkin controversy sufficiently demonstrates their lack of sincerity. To expect to learn particular details of teachings and events in the life and ministry of William Branham from such men would be no different from what someone described as trying to learn

Medieval History from someone who has only watched Robin Hood.

Thankfully there is a reliable and qualified person to help us understand details of dates with regards the Mystery Cloud event. Owen Jorgensen. He spent over 23 years researching on Branham's life and has chronicled a most detailed biography in a six-part book series. I regard Jorgensen as an important authority on this matter. The following is an excerpt from an article he authored. It is reproduced here with his kind permission.

●●●

Owen Jorgensen speaks

There has been some misunderstanding concerning the photographing of the mysterious Cloud over Arizona and the actual time when the seven angels came to William Branham. The pictures of the mysterious Cloud that appeared in the May 17, 1963 issue of Life Magazine were taken on the evening of February 28, 1963. After hearing some of William Branham's statements about this Cloud and about the pictures that were taken of it, many people (myself included) assumed he was hunting on February 28, the angels met him in the morning, and the supernatural Cloud was photographed in the evening over the same spot. However, that is not what the facts indicate, nor is it exactly what William Branham said.

During my research into this topic, I contacted Arizona's Game and Fish Department. Melissa Swain, who is their librarian, sent me a copy of the 1963 Arizona hunting regulations for javelinas. In 1963 the hunting season for javelinas began on Friday, March 1, and ended on Sunday, March 10. Since William Branham said he shot his javelina the day before the angels met him, if we put him out there hunting on the same day the mysterious Cloud was photographed, that would mean he was illegally hunting on the 27th and 28th of February. Speaking from my 23 years of researching this man's life, I can guarantee you he respected the law....

However, I don't just have circumstantial evidence. William Branham actually said he was not hunting in the Sunset Peak area on the same day the mysterious Cloud was photographed. Three months after the seven angels met him, while speaking at a house meeting in Tucson, he told his audience about the day when he first saw the pictures of the mysterious Cloud in Life Magazine. He said:

> ...Right there was them angels just as plain as they could be, setting right there in that picture. You see? I looked to see when it was, and-was time-same-about day or two before, or, day or two after I was up there. I looked where it was at-northeast of Flagstaff-or Prescott, which is below Flagstaff. Well, that's just where we was at, (see?) just exactly.[17]

This statement tells us that he knew from reading the article in Life Magazine that the pictures of that mysterious Cloud were not taken on the same day the seven angels met him. Speaking impromptu to that

---

[17] In the sermon *Come Follow Me,* 63-0601.

audience (six or seven weeks after he read the article in Life Magazine), he couldn't remember if the mysterious Cloud was photographed before or after he was hunting near Sunset Peak, but he knew for sure it was not the same day. At the same time it was clear to him that the mysterious Cloud pictured in Life Magazine looked exactly like what he saw on the morning of March 8 when the seven angels left him and rose into the sky.

So how did such a misconception concerning these events get started? It was the result of our misunderstanding of other things William Branham said that connected the mysterious Cloud over Flagstaff with the seven angels that met him near Sunset Peak…

In his sermon **Standing in the Gap**, preached in Jeffersonville, Indiana, on July 23, 1963, he said:

> How many saw, "A mysterious Cloud in the sky?" You see the hands. And now the Life Magazine picked it up, and I have the-the article here this morning, in the Life Magazine, of-to show. Now here it is-the same time I was there. See the pyramid of the Cloud? I was standing just below this. And there, see the distinctive angel on the right-hand side? See the pointed wing of it? Just exactly what was said. And here it's in the view of Mexico and different places from where they took the picture.

This certainly sounds like he is saying he was standing directly below this Cloud when it was being photographed. But that can't be what he is saying because the mysterious Cloud was photographed at least a hundred miles northwest of Sunset Peak. Is William Branham making something up? No he isn't. The answer is obvious when you compare this statement with the one I quoted previously. Look more closely at what he said in **Come Follow Me**. Referring to the pictures of the mysterious Cloud in Life Magazine, he said, "I looked to see when it was, and-was time-same-about day or two before, or, day or two after I was up there." You see, he is using the term "same time" in a slightly broader sense than what we originally assumed. He means that it all happened in the span of about a week (as opposed to two events happening months or even years apart). Notice he does the same thing with the location where the mysterious Cloud was photographed. He said, "I looked where it was at-northeast of Flagstaff-or Prescott, which is below Flagstaff. Well, that's just where we was at, (see?) just exactly." Here again he is using location in a broader sense, meaning that it happened in the same area of Arizona where he went hunting (as opposed to the mysterious Cloud appearing over, say, Tallahassee, Florida, or San Pablo, Brazil, or anywhere else in the world, for that matter. The world is a big place when compared to a 30-mile-long Cloud). At this point a critic might suggest that somehow William Branham saw this Cloud, either in person or in a newspaper article, and then made up a story to match its mysterious nature. That scenario doesn't fit the facts either. First of all, the Cloud wasn't seen from Tucson where William Branham was at when it appeared, nor to my knowledge were there any photographs of it published prior to the ones in Life Magazine (which William Branham didn't see until after the May 17th issue was released). Furthermore, William Branham had a vision of this event three months before it happened, which he announced and described in detail in his sermon, ***Is this the sign of the end, sirs?*** (62-1230E.) After seeing that vision he still was not sure how many angels would come to him, but he knew there would be at least five.

Consider this: only one time in the history of the world was there ever a cloud-like object photographed in the stratosphere, and that was on February 28, 1963 in the sky above central Arizona. Isn't it interesting that this mysterious Cloud (which scientifically can't exist at that altitude) just happened to look like the head of Jesus looking down on our world; and isn't it interesting that it just happened to appear in the same location and at the same time (broadly speaking) that William Branham said seven angels met him. A coincidence? I don't think so.

●●●

In all this confusion of trying to find fault, one problem is manifest – failing to *hear* right!

In Houston, Texas, in January of 1950, an amazing photograph was taken by the Douglas Studios. In the photograph, there appeared a halo-like Light above the head of Rev. William Branham. The negative was taken to George J. Lacy, Examiner of Questioned Documents for the FBI. His department was asked to determine whether or not the light could have been the result of improper exposure, developing or retouching. This investigation served to completely authenticate the fact that the unusual brightness was definitely caused by a light striking the negative. Mr. Lacy was quoted as saying, "Rev. Branham, you will die like all other mortals, but as long as there is a Christian civilization, your picture will live on."

(www.williambranhamhomepage.org/lhoust.htm)

8.
Hearing the voice of God

"But ye believe not, because ye are not of my sheep, as I said unto you. My sheep hear my voice, and I know them, and they follow me"

Joh.10:26-27

Paul was once a Pharisee, wholly devoted to the law of Moses. So committed was he that he persecuted what then was perceived a cult of Jesus and appeared to be breaking the Laws of Moses.

Saul, as he was called then, did not persecute the church with malicious intent. He was convinced that he was doing God a service. In his letter to believers at Philippi he recounted of his past life; *"as touching the law, a Pharisee; concerning zeal, persecuting the church; touching the righteousness which is in the law, blameless"* (Phi.3:5-7).

Like other Pharisees Saul believed that Jesus could not be the messiah because he disobeyed the Laws of God as given to Moses. Saul had to do God some service by trying to put to an end activities of the growing cult.

The conversion of Saul

One day he was all set to go to Damascus with his men when something astonishing happened; something that would not only change

Saul's life but the history of Christianity! Acts 9:3 recounts the event:

*"And as he journeyed, he came near Damascus: and suddenly there shined round about him a light from heaven: And he fell to the earth, and heard a voice saying unto him, Saul, Saul, why persecutest thou me?... And the men which journeyed with him stood speechless, **hearing a voice**, but seeing no man."*

That was the voice of the Lord Jesus. Saul realised that his intellectual doctrines and efforts had actually been fighting the God he thought he was serving. He repented of his sins, read the scriptures anew and realised that Jesus Christ was actually the fulfilment of what Moses and all the prophets spoke about. He wrote many epistles in which he expounded the teachings and ministry of Christ. He expounded how Christ was never at variance with the Law but instead its fulfilment.

In Galatians 5:14 Paul wrote, *"For all the law is fulfilled in one word, even in this; Thou shalt love thy neighbour as thyself."*

Now, let us look at how Paul one

day narrated his testimony of conversion. His words have been used by some Bible critics to state that Scripture contradicted itself, contrary to its claim of being divinely inspired. Paul was narrating the testimony of his conversion before authorities when he said:

*"they that were with me saw indeed the light, and were afraid; but **they heard not the voice** of him that spake to me"* (Act.22:7).

Note that the record of Paul's words in Acts 22:7 seem to be inconsistent with the report in Acts 9:3 wherein it is stated that the men with Paul had only seen a light but did not hear the voice that spoke to Paul. Is this an error in the Bible? Was Paul lying?

Well, anyone spiritual, with eyes to see and ears to hear the speaking of the Spirit, should perceive that the men with Saul only heard a sound of someone speaking but could not distinctly make out what words were being spoken. When God's visitation and words are directed at you, even when you are in a crowd, His Word and power can isolate you. You will be able to see, hear, and understand the message.

Daniel

Remember Daniel. One day he was with some people when they heard and experienced a quake. The men were afraid and ran away but the spiritual one among them, Daniel, was actually experiencing a vision of an angel coming to give him a message (Dan.10:7-9). A similar incident happened to the Lord when the people with Him heard a thunder but Himself heard the speaking of God (Joh.12:28-29). Here we learn that God can speak and one person may either hear nothing or simply become aware of something they can't comprehend, whilst another person for whom the message of God is intended can hear the voice distinctly. Thus, the men with Saul were surely aware of something supernatural happening as they could see the light. They heard the sound of some voice speaking but they just could not make out the words. To them the voice was inaudible.

What happened to the men with Paul makes a good example of what often happens whenever God speaks to a people: A lot wind up in only hearing *a voice* but not grasping *the voice* – the real essence or purpose of the message. So, like the Scripture says in Matthew 13:13, *"in hearing* (a voice) *they hear not* (the voice)."

Hearing voices of prophets every Sabbath

What happened to the men with Paul is what happened to the Jews who gathered every Sabbath to hear voices of the prophets read out of Scripture but yet never perceiving the fulfillment of the prophecies in Christ – *"because they knew him not, nor yet the voices of the prophets which are read every Sabbath day, they have fulfilled them in condemning him"* (Act.13:27).

But, how could they have heard when Grace was not given to them for their eyes to be opened to the revelation of the Truth. Clearly, if it had not been that supernatural encounter, Saul would have continued in darkness yet supposing he was some great scholar exposing and punishing those in error. For him to see the Truth and be set free from the traditions of the Law it took the power of God. When he became born again he counted all things he had earned in his past religious life as dung – *"Yea doubtless, and I count all things but loss for the excellency of the knowledge of Christ Jesus my Lord: for whom I have suffered the loss of all things, and do count them but dung, that I may win Christ"* (Phi.3:8).

9.

That every mouth may be stopped

"For that they hated knowledge, and did not choose the fear of the LORD: They would none of my counsel: they despised all my reproof. Therefore shall they eat of the fruit of their own way, and be filled with their own devices"

Pro.1:29-31

Adam and Eve were a perfect creation of God. Their bodies were made from the dust of the ground and so they had to be sustained by the *bread* of the ground – "*As for the earth, out of it cometh bread*" (Job 28:5). Thus, "*out of the ground made the LORD God to grow every tree that is pleasant to the sight, and good for food*" (Gen.2:9). But the spirit of life in man did not come from the ground; it came from the Word of Life, which was God, and hence *man could not live by bread alone* (Mat.4:4).

Man had to live by "*every word that proceedeth out of the mouth of God*" (Mat.4:4b). So, it wasn't enough for Eden to only have natural trees; "*the Tree of Life* [was] *also in the midst of the garden*"(Gen.2:9).

The Word was the power, anointing, and presence of God. Just like it once caused a dry and dead stick (rod) of Aaron to bud with leaves and fruits, it also gave life to man in Eden (Num.17:7-8).

In the garden of Eden was peace,

love, joy, and fellowship with God. The man and his woman walked in the way of the Tree of Life, the perfect will of God.

Now, although man was a grown up human being who knew that there was an alternative life of disobedience, God did not provide him a list of commandments - *thou shalt not steal, thou shalt not kill, thou shall not commit adultery*, and so on. There was no need for that. Two reasons.

First, because the giving of (and emphasizing of obedience to) laws is only useful in an environment where requirements or regulations are abrogated. Like apostle Paul wrote, "*the law is not made for a righteous man, but for the lawless and disobedient, for the ungodly and for sinners, for unholy and profane, for murderers of fathers and murderers of mothers, for manslayers*" (1 Tim.1:9).

Second, commanding a person to abstain from a sin (e.g. fornication) for which he is not concerned about will only work to arouse the curiosity about the sin. Does this mean a law of *thou shalt not commit fornication* would be wrong in itself? Not so, but like the Scripture says, *"Is the law sin? God forbid. Nay, I had not known sin, but by the law: for I had not known lust, except the law had said, Thou shalt not covet"* (Rom.7:7).

We can therefore say that *"by the law is the knowledge of sin"* (Rom.3:20).

Weakness of the flesh

One can never serve God in the flesh. The flesh is so weak that even when a person knows the right thing to do, he may still be tempted to do wrong (Rom.7:22-23). The flesh is governed by feelings and *want* for more (Ecc.1:7-8). It finds the ways and laws of God to be contrary to its appetites. It is for this reason that good and righteous as it was, the handwriting of Old Testament ordinances *"was against us"* and *"was contrary to us"* (Col.2:14). The law was contrary to the carnal desires of our flesh. When David sinned with Bathsheba and his sin was exposed, he cried to God: *"Behold, I was shapen in iniquity, and in sin did my mother conceive me"* (Psa.51:5).

But, someone may ask, why did God create us with the weak flesh which made Eve give in to temptation? Well, the flesh can only be influenced by what the mind has become obsessed with. Until it becomes an obsession, the mind still has strength to resist what is wrong. Eve had the opportunity not to commit her mind to what the Serpent was suggesting. But continued company and communion with the Serpent opened the curtains of her mind to iniquity. Apostle James admonished: *"Let no man say when he is tempted, I am tempted of God: for God cannot be tempted with evil, neither tempteth he any man: But **every man is tempted, when he is drawn away of his own lust, and enticed**. Then when lust hath conceived, it bringeth forth sin: **and sin, when it is finished, bringeth forth death"** (Jam.1:13-15).

It is important to know that man, having been created in the image and likeness of God, possesses free will.

Free will

Free will is what makes life a reality. Without it, God would have had to program us to be automatically exhibiting obedience and worship. That would have made life no different from a fictitious drama! Even so, in His mercy and grace, God created man in a state of wisdom and truth and left it to him to choose which way to 'eat' from – *the way of the Tree of Life* or *the way of the Tree of Knowledge of Good and Evil.*

Eating the fruit of our Way

It was only wise for man to have chosen the provided way of his loving and caring creator. But the woman got deceived into error. Man identified with her sin in order to save her. So, they both had to partake of the fruit of the way they had chosen: *"For that they hated knowledge, and did not choose the fear of the LORD: They would none of my counsel: they despised all my reproof. Therefore shall they eat of the fruit of their own way, and be filled with their own devices"* (Pro.1:29-31).

As of the way *of* the Tree of Life, God closed it – *"So he drove out the man; and he placed* **at the east of the garden of Eden** *Cherubims, and a flaming sword which turned every way, to keep* **the way of the tree of life"** (Gen.3:24, cf. Eze.44:1-3).

Man rejected grace and chose the law so to speak. It was his own choice and God had to let the law take its full course to let him know that even when he knows a right thing to do, which the law requires, he still would be unable to do right by himself, so *"that every mouth may be stopped and all the world may become guilty before God"* (Rom. 3:19).

10.

Shadows

"And the LORD said unto Moses, Hew thee two tables of stone like unto the first: and I will write upon these tables the words that were in the first tables, which thou brakest"

Exo. 34:1

Moses was coming down from the mountain, after forty days of being in the presence of God.

First and second tables of stone

On the mountain God gave Moses the Ten Commandments engraved on stones. Notice that the stones had been prepared by God, and the writing was done by God – *"**the tables were the work of God**, and **the writing was the writing of God**, graven upon the tables"* (Exo.32:16).

On coming down the mountain, Moses found the people had committed a terrible sin of idol worship. This was merely forty days after the people had witnessed the manifestation of God on Mount Sinai. Moses could not stand the sight.

So angry was Moses that he broke the stones which God had given him. But the Lord was patient. He called up the prophet to receive new sets of stone. However, there was a new requirement to receiving the second tables – *"And the LORD said unto Moses, **Hew thee** two* *tables of stone like unto the first: and **I will write upon these tables the words that were in the first tables**, which thou brakest"* (Exo.34:1).

There are three important things to note about the second tables of stone in this verse.

First, the second tables of stone were prepared by man, Moses. This was unlike the first ones which *"were the work of God"* (Exo.32:16). Second, God did not change the writing on the second tables. He said, *"I will write upon these tables the words that were in the first tables."* Third, the stones were placed in a wooden box called the Ark of Covenant (Deu.10:5). This wooden box was overlaid with gold within and outside (Exo.25:10-11).

Now, *"all these things happened unto them for ensamples and they are written for our admonition, upon whom the ends of the world are come"* (1 Cor.10:11).

Prepared by man

God created man in His image and likeness (Gen.1:26-27, 5:1). But man fell in sin and the image and likeness of God in him was 'marred'. Thus, the children that were born of Adam and Eve were not in the pure *image* of God, so to speak; they were born in the marred image of Adam - *"And Adam lived an hundred and thirty years, and begat a son in his own likeness, after his image; and called his name Seth"* (Gen.5:2).

Adam and Eve having been made by the hand of God were like the first tables of stone on which God wrote His commandments; they were *"the work of God"*, made in His image and likeness. They were 'born' in the perfect will of God, so to speak. However, from the time of the Fall, mankind is born of the will of the flesh. Like David said in his prayer, *"I was shapen in iniquity, and in sin did my mother conceive me"* (Psa.51:5).

The Word written in our hearts

In due course, God sent His son, born of pure blood to redeem us back to God. Although 'hewed' (born and shapen) through the will of the flesh, God touched and transformed us when He put His Word in our hearts – ***"I will put my law** in their inward parts, **and write it in their hearts**; and will be their God, and they shall be my people"* (Jer.31:33).

Wooden box overlaid with gold

Although transformed and born again, the heart of a believer still dwells in a 'wooden ark', the mortal body.

The mortal body was conceived through the will of the flesh. However, the transforming power of God inside the heart enables a son of God to manifest *goldliness* (holiness) even outwardly. To this agrees the words of Scripture – "*But as many as received him, to them gave he* **power to become the sons of God**, *even to them that believe on his name: Which were* **born [again]**, *not of blood,* **nor of the will of the flesh**, *nor of the will of man, but of God*" (Joh.1:12-13).

So, man who was once fallen in iniquity is now given the Grace to be born again. It's a new covenant of Grace. Through the new birth we become "*sons of God*" and hence the image of God is restored in us.

But, what is this "*power*" that enables us to become sons of God? What exactly is the New Testament of Grace? Is it the doing away of the law so that we become lawless Christians who tolerate sinful living and wrong dressing in the name of "God is gracious and only looks at our hearts"?

11.

Overcoming by Grace

"That the righteousness of the law might be fulfilled in us, who walk not after the flesh, but after the Spirit"

Rom. 8:4

Him who introduced the New Testament of Grace had this to say about the law:

"Think not that I am come to destroy the law, or the prophets: I am not come to destroy, but to fulfil. For verily I say unto you, **Till heaven and earth pass, one jot or one tittle shall in no wise pass from the law, till all be fulfilled***. Whosoever therefore shall break one of these least commandments, and shall teach men so, he shall be called the least in the kingdom of heaven: but whosoever shall do and teach them, the same shall be called great in the kingdom of heaven"* (Mat.5:17-19).

Christ did not come to destroy the law. The law was good. The New Testament was never meant to destroy it but to fulfil it. But, how was it fulfilled? We will answer this question in the course of this message.

It is important to emphasise here that a very good law had been given to the Hebrews on Mount Sinai. The law among other things required children to obey their parents, and for married people to be faithful to their spouses (by not committing adultery). The law also forbade murder and idolatry. Surely, these were good laws!

Now good as these laws may have been, the flesh of man was too weak to fulfil them. Like apostle Paul wrote, *"we know that the law is spiritual, but I am carnal, sold under sin"* (Rom.7:14, cf.Psa.51:5). In other words, what the law required was *"against"* or *"contrary"* to what our flesh desired (Col.2:14).

Strangely, even when one knows the right thing to do, and the wrong thing to avoid, he or she may still crave for the wrong and find themselves regretting later on – *"For I delight in the law of God after the inward man: But I see another law in my members, warring against the law of my mind, and bringing me into captivity to the law of sin which is in my members"* (Rom.7:22-23).

Well, God in His mercy decided to make a new covenant which would enable man fulfil the righteous requirements of the law. Instead of His Word being on tables of stone, He would now write it on the tables of the flesh of the heart of man – *"**written** not with ink, but with the Spirit of the living God; **not in tables of stone, but in fleshly tables of the heart**"* (2 Cor.3:3).

Promise of a new covenant

Jeremiah prophesied: *"Behold, the days come, saith the LORD, that I will make a new covenant with the house of Israel, and with the house of Judah: Not according to the covenant that I made with their fathers in the day that I took them by the hand to bring them out of the land of Egypt; which my covenant they brake, although I was an husband unto them, saith the LORD"* (Jer.31:31).

What would be this new covenant? Would it be lawlessness, so that everyone enjoys living in sin? Not so. Remember that there was nothing wrong with the law. It was the flesh of man which was susceptible to sin and hence always broke the laws of God. Well, the words of the prophecy of Jeremiah continues to tell us what the new covenant would be:

"This shall be the covenant that I will make with the house of Israel; After those days, saith the LORD, **I will put my law in their inward parts, and write it in their hearts;** *and will be their God, and they shall be my people"* (v.33).

So, under the new covenant man would receive the Spirit of the Word in his heart and hence be able to overcome the flesh as he continued to yield to the power of the Word that would abide in him. This is plainly stated in the prophecy of Ezekiel: *"And I will put my spirit within you, and cause you to walk in my statutes, and ye shall keep my judgments, and do them"* (Eze.36:26).

So, according to the prophecies of Jeremiah and Ezekiel, we can define the new covenant of grace as the coming of the Spirit of the Word in the heart of man to enable him fulfil the righteous requirements of the law. Like the Scripture says, *"That the righteousness of the law might be fulfilled in us, who walk not after the flesh, but after the Spirit"*(Rom. 8:4).

Walking in the Spirit

When a person receives the spirit of the Word, he becomes free from the *letter* of the law. Such a person is born again, the Spirit lives in him and liberates him from the carnal desires of the flesh.

"O wretched man that I am! who shall deliver me from the body of this death?" Paul asked, and answered: *"I thank God through Jesus Christ our Lord. So then with the mind I myself serve the law of God; but with the flesh the law of sin".*

*"There is therefore now no condemnation to them which are in Christ Jesus, who walk not after the flesh, but after the Spirit. For **the law of the Spirit of life in Christ Jesus hath made me free from the law of sin and death.** For what the law could not do, in that it was weak through the flesh, God sending his own Son in the likeness of sinful flesh, and for sin, condemned sin in the flesh: **That the righteousness of the law might be fulfilled in us, who walk not after the flesh, but after the Spirit"** (Rom.7:24-8:4).

"Ye are not under the Law"

The Ten Commandments were given to address *"works of the flesh"*. In Galatians 5:19 the works of the flesh have been listed:

- Adultery and fornication
- Idolatry
- Hatred
- Murders
- Emulations
- Drunkenness
- Wrath
- etcetera

When someone receives the Spirit of God, they cease to walk *after* (i.e. to be led by) the flesh. The Spirit of God in their hearts leads them and gives them power over sin. For this reason *"There is therefore now no condemnation to them which are in Christ Jesus, who walk not after the flesh, but after the Spirit"* (Rom.8:1).

So, as a believer, *"walk in the Spirit, and ye shall not fulfil the lust of the flesh"* (Gal.5:16). It follows that when you don't fulfil the lust of the flesh (for example, adultery) there is no need to give you a law against the work of the flesh (for example, *"Thou shalt not commit adultery"*). To this agrees the words of Scripture when it says that *"if ye be led of the Spirit,* **ye are not under the law"** (Gal.5:18).

The Spirit fills a believer with true love for God. If someone truly loves God, he or she can never use the name of the Lord in vain; he or she can never worship idols; he or she will never wait for a particular day of the week to worship God. No, he or she doesn't need to see *'a man who picked sticks on Sabbath'* be stoned to death in order to emphasize the importance of gathering for church on a Sabbath day. The desire for God is so much in him that he often spends time alone with God in prayer, fasting, and meditating on the Word, and also seizes any opportunity to fellowship with saints.

No boasting in Grace

The victory a child of God has when he

or she walks in the Spirit is not of *works*. His holiness does not proceed from what he tries to do in order to avoid punishment from God. What he does flows from the love he has for God and his brethren.

A believer is dead to the flesh and it is the Spirit of Christ living and manifesting in his life. This means that all good works that may proceed from the life of that person are resulting from the working of the Spirit that dwells in him – *"For **we are his workmanship**, created in Christ Jesus **unto good works**, which God hath before ordained that we should walk in them"* (Eph.2:10).

So, our righteousness can only come by resting in faith in the power that works in us. There can therefore be no boasting of works of righteousness that manifest in our lives. The good works that may manifest in us are not a result of our carnal efforts. We have faith in the God that saved us from our sins and we live surrendered lives to His will, and hence He works and lives in us both to will and to do good things – "*For it is God which worketh in you both to will and to do of his good pleasure*" (Phi.2:13).

It goes without saying that because we are merely the handiwork of God, there is no place of boasting! "*Where is boasting then? It is excluded. By what law? Of works? Nay, but by the law of faith*" (Rom.3:27).

12.

Throw away the sticks

"When that which is perfect is come, then that which is in part shall be done away"

1 Cor. 13:10

Old Testament laws were harsh. A troublesome, disobedient, and drunkard child, who was a heartache to his parents, was to be killed by stoning. He that smote another person to death was to be killed as well. Adultery likewise was punishable by death.

Modern societies would deem such laws to have been cruel. That is expectedly so when one looks at Old Testament societies through the lens of modern societies.

When looked at on a larger or global scale, modern societies have improved mannerisms and relations between human beings. In ancient times, societies were very uncivilised, brutal, and wicked.

It is important to know that since the since the Fall of mankind in Eden, human societies rebelled against morality and became reprobates. The mind of man was evil continually. Murder, adultery, battles and wars, and despicable pagan practices such as the sacrificing of children into flames of fire, characterised nations.

God had not forsaken mankind. It was mankind using free will to govern himself. However, God was silently working with and among a few people. There had to be a starting point to restore order. There was Noah and then Shem, and down through Abraham until a nation of Israel was established.

As God worked on the people of Israel, He guarded them from wrong influences of other nations by forbidding them to intermingle with other races. God had actually also used Israel on many occasions to destroy those nations which were completely sold to wickedness – *"for the wickedness of these nations the LORD thy God doth drive them out from before thee"* (Deu.9:5).

Israelites had entered into a covenant of righteousness with God. Whenever they broke that covenant and became lawless like other nations, God treated them just like He did the pagan nations.

Offenders of the law received stiff

punishment. This was to instil fear in others and prevent them from wrongdoing.

Observance of Sabbath days, festivals, and various other ceremonial laws was essential for keeping a nation in order and helping the carnal mind to conform and reform. This was not the perfect way but a necessary process in God's plan of restoration.

That period of time in Jewish history when Israelites lived by the law was like a time of elementary school for a young child. During that period a child is subjected to discipline and regularity until he is grown to appreciate the required concepts.

Counting sticks

In elementary school I was taught counting using sticks. Every day we repeated the counting process of saying *one, two, three...*

It is interesting to note that our young minds took the sticks to be numbers themselves. If a shorter stick was counted as *one* and the longer one *two,* counting starting with the longer stick was an abrogation of mathematics to our young minds. Well, teacher did not bother to correct our perception because *"precept must be upon precept…line upon line; here a little, and there a little"* (Isa.28:10).

Growing up a little older, we were able to count without the aid of sticks. We threw away the sticks!

No, we were not disrespecting our nursery school teacher and neither were we breaking any law of mathematics. Actually our teacher would have been proud of us to see us counting without the aid of sticks. He would have known that the lessons had fulfilled their purpose.

So, throwing away the sticks did not amount to throwing away arithmetic because the sticks were only objects pointing to the real concept of numbers! Once the concept was grasped, the objects had little or no use at all!

This example of sticks illustrates the

difference between serving God under the law and under the covenant of grace.

When the Perfect comes

A child can only use sticks for a certain period of time. The use of sticks has its lifespan so to speak. That *lifespan* of using sticks is only 'in part' of greater or 'perfect' lessons to come. However, "*when that which is perfect is come, then that which is in part shall be done away*" (1 Cor.13:10). Similarly, when Christ came preaching the gospel of the New Testament, He did not come to contradict Moses or the Torah as Jewish rabbis today still think. He came to fulfil the law. "*Think not that I am come to destroy the law, or the prophets. I am not come to destroy, but to fulfil*" the Lord said (Matt.5:17). Those with eyes to see and ears to hear could perceive that in Christ was the very Spirit that anointed Moses. When He spoke, although they could not fully comprehend a number of things they heard, they were still able to discern the life of the Word in the ministry of Jesus.

The law was a *"schoolmaster"* to bring people to Christ (Gal.3:24). The practices of the law were *objects* which pointed to the **real** thing to come. And just as arithmetic is not in the objects of "sticks" used for counting so is the righteousness of God not in those works of the law. Therefore, *"do not let anyone judge you by what you eat or drink, or with regard to a religious festival, a New Moon celebration or a Sabbath day. These are a* **shadow** *of the things that were to come;* **the reality**, *however, is* **found in Christ"** (Col.2:16-17, NIV).

13.

How camest thou in?

"And to her was granted that she should be arrayed in fine linen, clean and white: for the fine linen is the righteousness of saints"

Rev.19:8

As we see end-time prophecies get fulfilled, one cannot help but think that we are living in borrowed time. What is going on around the world, especially among superpower nations, brings to mind the seven visions William Branham had in 1933. These visions, he said, would be fulfilled before the coming of the Lord Jesus:

The **first vision** was that Mussolini would invade Ethiopia and that the nation would "fall at his steps"…The **next vision** foretold that an Austrian by the name of Adolph Hitler would rise up as dictator over Germany, and that he would draw the world into war...The third vision was in the realm of world politics for it showed me that there would be three great ISMS – Fascism, Nazism, Communism, but that the first two would be swallowed up into the third. The voice admonished, "WATCH RUSSIA, WATCH RUSSIA. Keep your eye on the King of the North." The **fourth vision** showed the great advances in science that would come after the second world war. It was headed up in the vision of a plastic bubble-topped car that was running down beautiful highways under remote control so that people appeared seated in this car without a steering wheel and they were playing some sort of a game to amuse themselves. The **fifth vision** had to do with the moral problem of our age, centering mostly around women...She adopted men's clothing and went into a state of undress…In the **sixth vision** there arose up in America a most beautiful, but cruel woman. She held the people in her complete power…The last and **seventh vision** was wherein I heard a most terrible explosion. As I turned to look I saw nothing but debris, craters, and smoke all over the land of America.[18]

When you read about what happened to Ethiopia at the hands of Mussolini, the advent of Hitler and the second war, and the inventions of egg-shaped bubble driverless vehicles which recently made headlines in news around the world, you and I should know that William Branham's prophecies were not a "Made in Nigeria" charismatic drama. Among those who have followed his ministry and the messages he preached, there is an excitement of talking about current events in the light of the seven visions, especially concerning the sixth and seventh visions. On the other hand, there is a world of pentecostals who know next to nothing concerning "*things that are to be*". Their "*watchmen*" are busy entertaining them with sermons about 'getting rich' and 'positive thinking'

---

[18] William Branham in *Exposition of the Seven Church Ages,* 1960.

when they are supposed to be in tears of repentance.

Now, for those who have received the end-time prophetic word, excitement shouldn't be about the knowledge of the prophecies. It is important to know that during the First Advent of Jesus Christ, the chief priests and scribes had known about the prophecy of the coming of the messiah but that didn't amount to making them partakers of its fulfilment. The fulfilment was only revealed to those whose lives were worthy of God's promises. Remember the shepherds? Remember Anne the Prophetess who served God with prayers and fasting? Remember Simeon, a devout believer who earnestly waited for the coming of the Lord? The lives of these people are examples for us to know that only those with a personal relationship with God shall experience the power that shall transform and translate the believers in the Rapture. It is one thing to find yourself gathered among believers but quite another to be sure of your place in His calling

Called to the 'Wedding'

Our calling in Christ is like an invitation to a wedding ceremony where every person has to dress up accordingly for the occasion. In this wedding ceremony we feast on God's Word. We feed on that Word not to get puffed up with knowledge about *this* and *that* mystery, but that our lives be transformed to manifest the life of Christ. The question each one of us should ask is, since the Lord called me and revealed His Word to me, what manner of life have I lived? Have I lived a fruitful Christian life or I have been ever learning but never coming to spiritual maturity (2 Tim.3:7)?

See, what will take us into the Rapture is not just knowing that there is *a* certain prophecy about to be fulfilled, but having a life that manifests the life of God's Word. The Lord Jesus once spoke a parable (in Mat. 22:9-13) that strikes a chord with this message:

"[the] *servants went out into the highways, and gathered together all as many as they found, both bad and good: and the wedding was furnished with guests. And when the king came in to see the guests, he saw there a man which had not on a wedding garment: And he saith unto him, Friend, **how camest thou in** hither not having a wedding garment? And he was speechless. Then said the king to the servants, Bind him hand and foot, and take him away, and cast him into outer darkness; there shall be weeping and gnashing of teeth.*"

Surely, different people have come into the fellowship of saints in different ways. For some it's been through a true conviction of Truth, and for others, they are in church to practice a social norm. There are many believers who found themselves in church simply because they were born and raised in a family of Christians. However, a true believer is one who has received the revelation of God's Word. It is God's Word which is our right clothing. Any other dressing – social norm, tradition, religious opinions – are not the right garments!

Your dressing testifies of your life

Physically speaking, what we dress exhibits our manner of life and can also portray our beliefs.

"God doesn't mind about what I dress outwardly because it's my heart which matters" is a common excuse of women who dress inappropriately and yet want to call themselves Christians. If dressing really never matters, we should ask ourselves why it mattered to saints of old in the Bible. In Genesis 35:1-4, the household of Jacob, upon being called by God, changed their garments and also removed their earrings. In the New Testament we also see an emphasis on modest dressing: *"In like manner also, that women adorn themselves in modest apparel, with shamefacedness and sobriety; not with broided hair, or gold, or pearls, or costly array"* (1 Tim. 2:9).

Here in my country of Zambia, when it is at a funeral gathering, women want to dress modestly. Those with short skirts or tight trousers carry a piece of cloth called *Chitenge* which they use to wrap around themselves to cover up their immodest outfits. Why is there this foolishness of revering the *dead* with proper dressing but yet dishonouring oneself's body to the *living* public?

Some women dress immodestly on purpose to cause men's heads to turn, and others are simply caught in the wind of what is trending. It is important to be aware that in this life you are following someone. Yes, there is someone who influences your beliefs and manner of life.

Many women don't know that many outfits they put on were specially designed to make them sexually attractive. Most modern female outfits are designed on purpose to make conspicuous certain parts of a woman's body which attract males – the breasts, the thighs, the hips, and the buttocks. One thing this has achieved is to portray women as sex objects. Those who are wise should discern that there is an immoral objective and sales-target to be accomplished behind an immodest outfit.

In my culture it used to be a taboo for a woman to expose her breasts or thighs. However, things have changed. Western culture has so much influenced our society that many African women have to buy hair that looks like a white man's, many bleach their skin to look lighter, and others twist their accent to sound American.

On TV young people watch how 'more civilised' societies dress, and

what have we got, a society of young ladies who wear in public clothes which their grandparents only wore in the bedroom, and young men who don't know where their waistline is to hold the belt!

In speaking about dressing and how it can express who is leading you in life, or what you believe in, I am reminded of Nelson Mandela.

Mandela's kaross at Rivonia Trial

Nelson Mandela once gave a dramatic expression of what dressing entails and this angered and threatened the Apartheid-whites.

This was at the famous *Rivonia trial* when he was sentenced to imprisonment. In his autobiography he recounted:

> I entered the court that Monday morning wearing a traditional Xhosa leopard-skin kaross instead of a suit and tie. The crowd of supporters rose as one and with raised clenched fists shouted *"Amandla!"* and *"Ngawethu!"* The kaross electrified the spectators…I had chosen traditional dress to emphasise the symbolism that I was a black African walking into a white man's court. I was literally carrying on my back the history, culture, and heritage of my people… When I was on my way back to the cell, a very nervous white warder said that the commanding officer, Colonel Jacobs,

had ordered me to hand over the kaross. I said,
"You can tell him that he is not going to have it." [19]

Believers need to know that through the ages, true God-called people have only had one kind of dressing – the revelation of God's Word. To borrow Mandela's words, our dressing should bear *"the history, culture, and heritage"* of God's people over the ages. Anytime we try to adopt some new fashion of the compromised ecclesiastical system we should remember that we are going back to a system that imprisoned us into tradition and dogma. And is it not the case that many believers who were delivered from Babylon came out of the system only to turn around and end up in a more serious 'Babel' of confusion? When you look at their spiritual dressing, it certainly is not the required one and one day someone will have to answer the question, *"how camest thou in hither?"* There is ONLY ONE WAY to entering God's fold and that is through

---

[19] Nelson Mandela in *Long Walk to Freedom, 1994.* Backbay Books, New York.

the revelation of His Word. Any other religious method is false.

Nelson Mandela gave his life completely to the struggle for the freedom of South Africans. The struggle became his obsession. Other people who felt a responsibility to fight against the Apartheid system found themselves living the same kind of life. They went in and out of jail but that did not matter to them. Something – a great cause – kept the flames of their spirits lit. At one moment, recounts Mandela, they were imprisoned and discouraged. But someone started singing a song and a 'revival' started:

We sang at the top of our lungs, and it kept our spirits high. One time, Masabalala Yengwe…the son of a Zulu labourer…draped himself with a blanket, rolled up a newspaper to imitate an assegai, and began to stride back and forth reciting the lines from the praise song [this was a song in praise of Shaka, the great king of Zulus in southern Africa – Ed]. All of us, even those who did not understand Zulu were entranced. Then he paused dramatically and called out the lines *"Inyon' edl' ezinye! Yath' isadl' ezinye, yadl' ezinye!"* The lines liken Shaka to a great bird of prey that relentlessly slays its enemies. At the conclusion of these words, pandemonium broke out. Chief Luthuli, who until then had remained quite, sprang to his feet, and bellowed, *"Ngu Shaka lowo!"* (That is Shaka!), and then began to dance and chant. His movements electrified us, and we all took to our feet…Some moved gracefully, others resembled frozen mountaineers trying to shake off the cold, but all danced with enthusiasm and emotion. Suddenly there were no Xhosas or Zulus, no Indians or Africans, no rightists or leftists, no religious or political leaders; we were all nationalists and patriots bound together by a love of our common history, our culture, our country, and our people. In that moment, something stirred deep inside all of us, something strong and intimate, that bound us to one another. In that moment we felt the hand of the great past that made us what we were and the power of the great cause that linked us all together.[20]

When I read these words, I thought about what happens when someone receives a true conviction of the Holy Spirit. The conviction in his heart becomes his life and he gets free from tradition. And when people are confronted with reality, their false traditions crumble and fall apart. This reminds me of one time when a Jehovah Witness once approached me asking about why in our church everyone

---

[20] ibid. p.277-278.

prays together in a pentecostal way.

"Prayer should be quite and orderly" he chided. "How can God hear you when you are all making noise?"

I opened my Bible and read to him Ezra 3:11-13 which says that the people *"sang together by course in praising and giving thanks unto the LORD… many shouted aloud for joy so that the people could not discern the noise of the shout of joy from the noise of the weeping of the people: for the people shouted with a loud shout, and the noise was heard afar off."*

I asked the gentleman, "Do you think these were Jehovah Witnesses?"

When reality strikes

Religion makes people have two faces in life – one they exhibit when they are in church and another when they are truly themselves elsewhere. When at home watching soccer, for example, some people will scream and yell and dance in expressing their emotion. That's the real them! That's their life. It is filled with the 'spirit of football.' That's what they enjoy! Now, it goes without saying that a person whose mind has become obsessed with the Spirit of the Gospel also lives to the full expression of its joy.

It is interesting to know that when reality strikes, even the most traditional people discard their norms and yield to the emotion and cry of their spirits. This happened one day when some students at a college I once worked were trying to come up the building using an elevator. They were about five of them on their way to the eighth floor of the building when suddenly the elevator stopped and smoke started filling the cell. Panic and confusion set in. One student tried to dial my number as others started to scream. Then the Jehovah Witness, the Catholic, and the Seventh Day Adventist began to shout, calling on the name of Jesus. After narrating the incident to me, I said to the students, "Now, that was the real you praying. In that moment no one had the time to play with the rosary."

Dear saints, God has called us to sincerity. The Word was preached and we heard the voice of God. We entered into the fold of God through the one door of the revelation of His Word. That Word has transformed our hearts. What is in our hearts manifests outwardly and we become a light in the dark environments we find ourselves. *"I will greatly rejoice in the LORD, my soul shall be joyful in my God; for he hath clothed me with the garments of salvation, he hath covered me with the robe of righteousness"* (Isa. 61:10). Amen.

Other books by Andrew C. Phiri

ANSWERING THE QUESTION
Who created the Creator?

Free copies available while stocks last. Otherwise buy from book store. A simple search on the Internet will show you stores where the book is available.

WHY I BELIEVE GOD EXISTS
Discourse on the scientific evidence

FORBIDDEN THEOLOGY
Making sense of the Genesis story